SLOW COOKER RECIPE BOOK

SLOW COOKER RECIPE BOOK

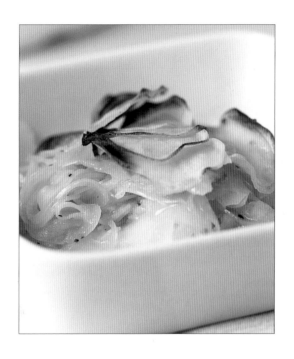

Nice and slow: over 60 mouthwatering meals
cooked with minimum effort but maximum flavour

CATHERINE ATKINSON

southwater

This edition is published by Southwater

Southwater is an imprint of Anness Publishing Ltd
Hermes House, 88–89 Blackfriars Road, London SE1 8HA
tel. 020 7401 2077; fax 020 7633 9499; info@anness.com

© Anness Publishing Ltd 2005

UK agent: The Manning Partnership Ltd
sales@manning-partnership.co.uk
UK distributor: Grantham Book Services Ltd
orders@gbs.tbs-ltd.co.uk
North American agent/distributor: National Book Network
www.nbnbooks.com
Australian agent/distributor: Pan Macmillan Australia
customer.service@macmillan.com.au
New Zealand agent/distributor: David Bateman Ltd
tel. (09) 415 7664; fax (09) 415 8892

Publisher: Joanna Lorenz
Editorial Director: Helen Sudell
Recipes: Catherine Atkinson, Jane Bamforth, Alex Barker, Valerie Barrett, Judy Bastyra,
Carole Clements, Joanna Farrow, Brian Glover, Nicola Graimes, Christine Ingram, Becky
Johnson, Lucy Knox, Marlene Spieler, Kate Whiteman, Rosemary Wilkinson, Jeni Wright
Photography: Karl Adamson, Steve Baxter, Nicki Dowey, Amanda Heywood, Janine Hosegood,
Don Last, William Adams-Lingwood, Craig Robertson, Bridget Sargeson, Sam Stowell
Designer: Nigel Partridge
Production Controller: Claire Rae

Previously published as part of a larger compendium: *The Slow Cooker Cookbook*

1 3 5 7 9 10 8 6 4 2

NOTES
Bracketed terms are for American readers.
For all recipes, quantities are given in both metric and imperial measures and,
where appropriate, measures are also given in standard cups and spoons.
Follow one set, but not a mixture, because they are not interchangeable.
Standard spoon and cup measures are level.
1 tsp = 5ml, 1 tbsp = 15ml, 1 cup = 250ml/8fl oz
Australian standard tablespoons are 20ml. Australian readers should use 3 tsp in
place of 1 tbsp for measuring small quantities of gelatine, cornflour, salt etc.
American pints are 16fl oz/2 cups. American readers should use 20fl oz/2.5 cups in
place of 1 pint when measuring liquids.
Medium (US large) eggs are used unless otherwise stated.

NUTRITIONAL INFORMATION
The nutritional analysis given for each recipe is calculated per portion (i.e. serving or
item), unless otherwise stated. If the recipe gives a range, such as Serves 4–6,
then the nutritional analysis will be for the smaller portion size i.e. 6 servings.
Measurements for sodium do not include salt added to taste.

Main front cover image shows Steak and Kidney Pie
with Mustard Gravy – for recipe, see page 46.

CONTENTS

INTRODUCTION

Long, slow cooking techniques have been used for centuries. From the earliest times, cooks discovered that meat roasted in the dying embers of the fire, or in a pot of gently bubbling stock suspended well above the flames, produced the tenderest results with rich, well-balanced flavours.

Cooking methods have developed and improved over the years, but no drastic changes were seen until the reduction of staff employed in richer households meant that very few people still had a cook who would spend the entire day preparing food, thus leading to changes in the types of food prepared.

Along with the gradual introduction of controllable range cookers and, eventually, the introduction of modern gas and electric ovens came an increased demand for dishes requiring less cooking time. In the latter half of the 20th century, more women went out to work, and time-saving became all-important.

Food manufacturers thrived on the sale of prepared ingredients that could

Below: The gentle heat of the slow cooker means that delicate fish cooks beautifully.

reduce the number of hours spent in the kitchen. Canned and dried soups, dehydrated prepared vegetables, main meals and "instant" desserts were all the rage at the end of the 1960s and throughout the 1970s.

The rise and fall of the slow cooker

In the mid-1970s, the slow cooker was invented. It was originally designed for making baked beans and was marketed to the public as an appliance that would cook a wholesome meal unattended, ready to be served after a hard day's work. As such it caught the attention of those with busy working lives. It lived up to its promise, and busy working mothers, families and students soon discovered its delights. The slow cooker's popularity continued for a decade.

However, with the booming economy years in the late 1980s and 1990s, the demand for economical cuts of meat fell. They were replaced by lean prime cuts, such as chicken breast portions and beef steak, which were more suited to fast cooking methods, such as grilling, broiling and stir-frying. Time-saving

Above: Wonderfully warming soups are easy to make in a slow cooker.

appliances appeared on the scene, including the microwave – and with their arrival, many slow cookers were left to gather dust.

Changing attitudes

Towards the end of the 20th century and in the new millennium, there has been a change in attitudes towards food and a reverse in eating trends. Many people now demand natural food, with fewer artificial chemicals and more nutrients and flavour, rather than instant, quick-fix food. Genetically modified produce has not been welcomed and sales of organic food have rocketed, along with requests for less tender, tastier cuts of meat. Slow-simmered casseroles, home-made soups and traditional desserts are back in fashion, and so are slow cookers.

From tasty, wholesome family food to sophisticated entertaining, a slow cooker is a superb way to create wonderfully tender and flavour-packed meals. Its reputation for making delicious soups and succulent stews is well known, and the slow cooker is far more versatile than many people realize.

Because the slow cooker cooks gently, without the vigorous bubbling or fierce heat of some other cooking methods, delicate food, such as fish, fruit and vegetables, won't break up even after long cooking. Used as a bain-marie the slow cooker can produce divine creamy "baked" custards, the lightest sponge desserts, and tasty terrines and pâtés. The constant temperature makes it perfect for keeping party punches steaming hot and simmering preserves so that the flavours mingle, making ready-to-eat preserves that don't need to be left to mature.

There are many advantages to using a slow cooker. Not only does it produce delicious dishes with well-developed flavours, but once the food is in the slow cooker you can usually turn it on and forget about it. Because the slow cooker uses less electricity than a light bulb, it can also be left unattended.

Some slow cookers have timers that automatically switch to the warm setting when the food is cooked, and this is ideal for households who eat at different times. The remaining portions will still be deliciously moist for latecomers. As an added bonus, little steam or smell escapes from slow cookers.

Above: The slow cooker makes excellent steamed bread and fruit puddings.

You will be pleasantly surprised at the range of uses of the slow cooker. Although traditionally associated with cold weather foods, such as warming casseroles, soups and stews, you can also make delicious hot weather dishes, such as chilled pâtés and terrines, light fish dishes and summery Mediterranean-style pasta meals. The slow cooker really is invaluable when it is warm outside and you don't want to be confined to a steamy kitchen, with the oven pumping out heat. Simply switch on the slow cooker and leave it to it.

Using this book

This book is ideal for the first-time slow cooker user, as well as the more experienced slow cooker fan. It contains a wonderful selection of easy classic recipes that are sure to become household favourites. Step-by-step photographs show the key preparation stages of each recipe to give successful results every time.

Most recipes are based on a family of four people, but if you have a small or large slow cooker the quantities can easily be halved to serve two, or doubled for eight. All recipes have been thoroughly tested, but it is important to get to know your slow cooker, as times can vary from one model to another. After trying a few recipes, you will know whether your slow cooker is faster or slower, and you will be able to adjust the recipe cooking times you use for your own slow cooker accordingly.

Below: Pastry toppings for traditional pies are oven-cooked to retain their crispness.

Below: Individual servings can be cooked in single-portion ramekins in the slow cooker.

SLOW COOKER BASICS

The basic principle behind the slow cooker is that it cooks food very slowly at a low temperature. The heat gradually builds up and is then maintained at an even temperature throughout cooking, to give perfect, tender results. Slow cookers are very simple and economical to use. They have a low wattage that consumes about the same amount of electricity as a light bulb, which makes them environmentally friendly as well.

Choosing a slow cooker

There is a very wide selection of slow cookers available. They come in a range of sizes, shapes, colours and prices, and it is these factors that you will need to think about before you decide which type of slow cooker is right for you.

When slow cookers were first manufactured, the earthenware or ceramic pots were permanently fixed into the heat-resistant plastic or aluminium outer casing. While it is still possible to buy models made this way, most modern versions have a removable cooking pot that fits snugly into an inner metal casing. The heating elements are safely situated between the inner and outer casings. This newer style not only simplifies washing up, but allows the cooking pot to be lifted out and taken to the table as a serving dish. In addition, food can be browned in the oven or under the grill (broiler) without causing damage to the outer casing.

The heat-resistant lid may be made of toughened glass or ceramic. The former has the advantage of allowing you to monitor the food's cooking progress without lifting off the lid and losing heat and moisture, although this may be hindered to some extent by steam and condensation gathering on the inside of the lid.

The range of designs and colours of slow cookers has increased in recent years. The original round-shaped rustic cream and brown design with ceramic lid is still available, but alongside it you will now find much more contemporary-looking white, stainless steel and brightly coloured models that will fit well in a bright, modern kitchen.

Slow cookers may be round or oval in shape. Round ones are superb for cooking casseroles, steaming desserts and cooking cakes in round tins (pans), while the oval version is better for pot-roasted meats and for use with loaf tins (pans) and terrines.

The size of different slow cookers can vary enormously – from a small 600ml/1 pint/2½ cup cooking pot to a huge 6.5 litre/11¼ pint/26¼ cup one. Of all the sizes, the most popular size is probably 3.5 litres/6 pints/14¼ cups, which will enable you to cook a wide range of dishes and easily cater for four people. However, the smaller versions, intended for cooking just one or two portions at a time, are a great asset for single people and couples and take up less space in the kitchen. They are also perfect for making hot dips and fondues.

Below: Oval-shaped slow cookers are perfect for cooking certain types of food, such as pot-roasted joints of meat, long, loaf-shaped terrines, and small whole fish.

Temperature settings

The cooking temperatures and settings on slow cookers vary slightly from model to model. The most basic (but perfectly adequate) models have three settings: off, low and high. When the slow cooker is switched to low, the food will barely simmer, and at the highest setting it will cook at a simmer or even boil.

Other models have an additional medium setting and some also have an auto setting. The auto setting is thermostatically controlled, so that the cooking temperature builds up to high, maintains it for a short time, then automatically switches to low to maintain the heat. It normally takes about an hour for the slow cooker to reach the "high" temperature, but this depends on the quantity of food being cooked and its initial temperature.

Most slow cooker models also have a power indicator light that remains on constantly during cooking – although in a few models it may switch off to indicate that the optimum temperature has been reached, so check the instructions.

Using a new slow cooker

Every model of slow cooker varies slightly, so it is important to read the manufacturer's instructions carefully before using. Even when using the same settings, some cookers will cook slower or faster than others.

To cover all models of slow cooker, the recipes in this book offer a range of cooking times. Depending on whether your own model cooks more slowly or quickly, you will either need to use the longer or shorter timing, or somewhere in between. Once you have used your new cooker a few times, it will be easy to know at a glance which cooking time you need to use.

Preheating

Some slow cookers need to be preheated on high for 15–20 minutes before cooking. However, always check the instructions first because some models heat up quickly, making this step unnecessary, and the manufacturer may advise against heating the slow cooker when empty.

To preheat the slow cooker, place the empty cooking pot and lid in the slow cooker base and switch the temperature on to the high setting. While the slow cooker heats up, prepare the ingredients for the recipe.

Slow cooker care

Always remove any labels and tags from a new slow cooker, then wash the ceramic cooking pot well in hot soapy water, rinse and dry thoroughly.

After use, the slow cooker should be switched off before removing the ceramic cooking pot. If you don't want to wash the pot immediately after serving the food, it can be filled with warm water and left to soak for as long as necessary. However, do not immerse the entire pot in water for long periods of time because the base is usually porous and soaking may damage the pot. Very few cooking pots are dishwasher-proof, but it is worth checking the manufacturer's instructions; these should also inform you whether the cooking pot can be used on the stovetop or in the oven, microwave or freezer.

Never plunge the hot cooking pot into cold water immediately after use, or pour boiling water into an empty cold cooking pot. Subjecting it to a sudden change in temperature could cause it to crack. As with all electrical appliances, never immerse the outer casing in water or fill it with water. Nor should you use the metal inner casing without the ceramic cooking pot.

Scouring pads and abrasive cleaners will damage the outside of the cooker, so use a damp soapy cloth to clean it.

Above: *Smaller slow cookers intended for cooking just one or two portions at a time are an asset for single people and couples.*

During cooking, the cooking pot and lid will become very hot, so always use oven gloves when handling. The outer casing may also become hot after long cooking, so care should be taken when touching this, too.

The first few times you use a slow cooker, you may notice a slight odour. This is caused by the burning off of manufacturing residues, which is normal, and will lessen and disappear after time. After several months, the glaze on the cooking pot may become crackled; this is common with glazed stoneware and will not affect the slow cooker's efficiency.

Adapting your own recipes

Conventional recipes can be adapted for cooking in a slow cooker. The easiest way to adapt a recipe is to find a similar one in this book and use it as a guide to adapt the original recipe. As a general rule, the liquid content of a dish cooked conventionally can be reduced by as much as half in a slow cooker. Check towards the end of cooking time and add more hot liquid if necessary.

Tips for success

During cooking, steam will condense on the lid of the slow cooker, then slowly trickle back into the pot. This helps to form a seal around the lid, retaining heat, flavour and cooking smells. If possible, avoid lifting the lid during cooking because this will cause heat loss and lengthen the cooking time. Unless a recipe states otherwise, the slow cooker should be left undisturbed. There is no need to stir food frequently because the even cooking and low temperature help to prevent food from sticking or bubbling over. Should you need to lift the lid though, add an extra 15–20 minutes to the cooking time to make up for the heat lost.

If at the end of the cooking time the food is not quite ready, replace the lid and switch the slow cooker to high to speed up the cooking process. Once ready, many dishes can be kept hot for an hour or so without risk of spoiling, by switching the slow cooker to low.

Guide to cooking times

You can often introduce some flexibility to the total cooking time by adjusting the temperature setting. Certain foods, however, are only successful if cooked at the specified setting. Cakes, for example, should always be cooked on high for the entire cooking time, and pot-roasted meats and egg-based recipes should usually be started on high (or auto) for the first hour of cooking, then reduced. For dishes such as soups and casseroles, the cooking time may be shortened or extended to suit your needs by cooking on a higher or lower setting. As a rough guide, the cooking time on high is just over half that on low.

Low	Medium	High
6–8 hours	4–6 hours	3–4 hours
8–10 hours	6–8 hours	5–6 hours
10–12 hours	8–10 hours	7–8 hours

SOUPS AND APPETIZERS

The slow cooker truly excels when it comes to soup-making – the long, gentle cooking allows the flavours to develop fully over time, giving rich results. It is great for making appetizers too, particularly pâtés and terrines, which work exceptionally well. This chapter offers classic French onion soup with cheese croûtes, and seafood chowder for a hearty lunch to delicate Greek avgolemono for an elegant start to a meal. There is a pretty fish terrine, along with a spicy carrot dip and divine poached pears stuffed with cheese, which are perfect for a special dinner party.

FRENCH ONION SOUP with CHEESE CROÛTES

Probably the most famous of all onion soups, this hearty, warming dish was traditionally served as a sustaining early morning meal to the porters and workers of Les Halles market in Paris. Use large yellow Spanish onions for the best result.

3 Add the sugar and stir well. Cover again with the lid and folded dish towel and continue cooking on high for 4 hours, stirring two or three times, to ensure the onions are colouring evenly. At the end of this time, they should be a dark golden colour.

4 Sprinkle the flour over the onions and stir to mix. Next, stir in the vinegar followed by the brandy, then slowly blend in the wine. Stir in the stock and thyme and season with salt and pepper. Cook on high for a further 2 hours, or until the onions are very tender.

5 For the croûtes, place the bread slices under a low grill (broiler) and cook until dry and lightly browned. Rub the bread with the cut surface of the garlic and spread with mustard, then sprinkle the grated Gruyère cheese over the slices.

SERVES 4

40g/1½oz/3 tbsp butter
10ml/2 tsp olive oil
1.2kg/2½lb onions, peeled and sliced
5ml/1 tsp caster (superfine) sugar
15ml/1 tbsp plain (all-purpose) flour
15ml/1 tbsp sherry vinegar
30ml/2 tbsp brandy
120ml/4fl oz/½ cup dry white wine
1 litre/1¾ pints/4 cups boiling beef, chicken or duck stock
5ml/1 tsp chopped fresh thyme
salt and ground black pepper

For the croûtes
4 slices day-old French stick or baguette, about 2.5cm/1in thick
1 garlic clove, halved
5ml/1 tsp French mustard
50g/2oz/½ cup grated Gruyère cheese

1 Put the butter and olive oil in the ceramic cooking pot and heat on high for about 15 minutes until melted.

2 Add the onions to the pot and stir to coat well in the melted butter and oil. Cover with the lid, then place a folded dish towel over the top to retain all the heat and cook for 2 hours, stirring halfway through cooking time.

6 Turn the grill to high and cook the croûtes for 2–3 minutes, until the cheese melts, bubbles and browns. Ladle the soup into warmed bowls and float a Gruyère croûte on top of each. Serve straight away.

Nutritional information per portion: Energy 418Kcal/1747kJ; Protein 11.5g; Carbohydrate 51.8g, of which sugars 19.4g; Fat 15.9g, of which saturates 8.2g; Cholesterol 33mg; Calcium 209mg; Fibre 5.3g; Sodium 1195mg.

CARROT and CORIANDER SOUP

Root vegetables, such as carrots, are great for slow cooker soups. Their earthy flavour becomes rich and sweet when cooked slowly over a gentle heat and goes perfectly with robust herbs and spices, and their texture becomes beautifully smooth when puréed.

SERVES 4

450g/1lb carrots, preferably young
   and tender
15ml/1 tbsp sunflower oil
40g/1½oz/3 tbsp butter
1 onion, chopped
1 stick celery, plus 2–3 pale leafy tops
2 small potatoes, peeled
900ml/1½ pints/3¾ cups boiling
   vegetable stock
10ml/2 tsp ground coriander
15ml/1 tbsp chopped fresh coriander
   (cilantro)
150ml/¼ pint/⅔ cup milk
salt and ground black pepper

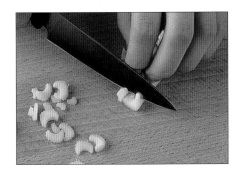

1 Trim and peel the carrots and cut into chunks. Heat the oil and 25g/1oz/2 tbsp of the butter in a pan and fry the onion over a gentle heat for 3–4 minutes until slightly softened. Do not let it brown.

2 Slice the celery and chop the potatoes, and add them to the onion in the pan. Cook for 2 minutes, then add the carrots and cook for a further 1 minute. Transfer the fried vegetables to the ceramic cooking pot.

3 Pour the boiling vegetable stock over the vegetables, then season with salt and ground black pepper. Cover the pot with the lid and cook on low for 4–5 hours until the vegetables are tender.

4 Reserve 6–8 tiny celery leaves from the leafy tops for the garnish, then finely chop the remaining celery tops. Melt the remaining butter in a large pan and add the ground coriander. Fry for about 1 minute, stirring constantly, until the aromas are released.

5 Reduce the heat under the pan and add the chopped celery tops and fresh coriander. Fry for about 30 seconds, then remove the pan from the heat.

6 Ladle the soup into a food processor or blender and process until smooth, then pour into the pan with the celery tops and coriander. Stir in the milk and heat gently until piping hot. Check the seasoning, then serve garnished with the reserved celery leaves.

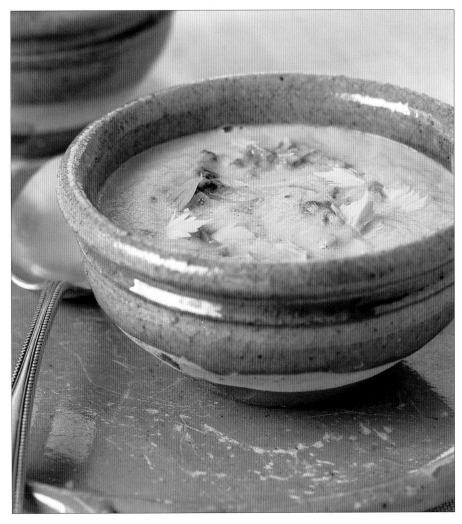

Nutritional information per portion: Energy 168Kcal/697kJ; Protein 3g; Carbohydrate 11.9g, of which sugars 9.2g; Fat 12.4g, of which saturates 6g; Cholesterol 24mg; Calcium 94mg; Fibre 3.1g; Sodium 758mg.

SPICY PUMPKIN SOUP

This stunning golden-orange soup has a smooth velvety texture, and a delicate taste, which is subtly spiced with cumin and garlic. Long, slow cooking really gives the flavours time to develop and come together to make a wonderful autumnal dish.

SERVES 4

900g/2lb pumpkin, peeled
   and seeds removed
30ml/2 tbsp olive oil
2 leeks, trimmed and sliced
1 garlic clove, crushed
5ml/1 tsp ground ginger
5ml/1 tsp ground cumin
750ml/1¼ pints/3 cups near-boiling
   chicken stock
salt and ground black pepper
60ml/4 tbsp natural (plain) yogurt, to serve
coriander (cilantro) leaves, to garnish

COOK'S TIP
To save time, reheat the soup on the
stovetop rather than in the slow cooker.

1 Using a sharp knife, cut the pumpkin into large chunks. Place the chunks in the ceramic cooking pot.

2 Heat the oil in a large pan and add the leeks and garlic. Cook gently until softened but not coloured.

3 Add the ginger and cumin to the pan and cook, stirring, for a further minute. Tip the mixture into the ceramic cooking pot, pour over the chicken stock and season with salt and black pepper.

4 Cover the slow cooker with the lid, switch to low and cook for 6–8 hours, or until the pumpkin is very tender.

5 Ladle the soup, in batches if necessary, into a food processor or blender and process until smooth. Return the soup to the rinsed out cooking pot, cover and cook on high for 1 hour, or until piping hot. Serve in warmed individual bowls, with a swirl of natural yogurt and a few coriander leaves.

Nutritional information per portion: Energy 89Kcal/372kJ; Protein 2.3g; Carbohydrate 6.2g, of which sugars 4.7g; Fat 6.3g, of which saturates 1.1g; Cholesterol 0mg; Calcium 75mg; Fibre 3.1g; Sodium 127mg.

WILD MUSHROOM SOUP

This robust, creamy soup is ideal for a simple lunch or supper, served with chunks of nutty wholegrain bread spread with fresh butter. The rich flavour and colour of the soup are further enhanced by the addition of dried wild mushrooms and a dash of Madeira.

SERVES 4

15g/½oz/¼ cup dried wild mushrooms,
   such as morels, ceps or porcini
600ml/1 pint/2½ cups hot chicken
   or vegetable stock
25g/1oz/2 tbsp butter
1 onion, finely chopped
1 garlic clove, crushed
450g/1lb button (white) or other
   cultivated mushrooms, trimmed
   and sliced
15ml/1 tbsp plain (all-purpose) flour
fresh nutmeg
1.5ml/¼ tsp dried thyme
60ml/4 tbsp Madeira or dry sherry
60ml/4 tbsp crème fraîche or
   sour cream
salt and ground black pepper
chopped fresh chives, to garnish

1 Put the dried mushrooms in a sieve (strainer) and rinse under cold running water to remove any grit, then place in the ceramic cooking pot. Pour over half of the hot chicken or vegetable stock and cover with the lid. Switch the slow cooker to the auto or high setting.

2 Place the butter in a large pan and melt over a medium heat. Add the chopped onion and cook for 5–7 minutes until softened and just golden.

3 Add the garlic and fresh mushrooms to the pan and cook for 5 minutes. Sprinkle over the flour, then grate some nutmeg into the mixture and add the thyme. Cook for 3 minutes more, stirring all the time, until blended.

4 Stir in the Madeira or sherry and the remaining stock, and season with salt and pepper. Bring to the boil, then transfer to the ceramic cooking pot. Cook for 1 hour, then switch to low or leave on auto and cook for a further 3–4 hours, or until the mushrooms are very tender.

5 Ladle the soup into a food processor or blender and process until smooth. Strain it back into the pan, pressing it with the back of a spoon to force the purée through the sieve.

6 Reheat the soup until piping hot, then stir in half the crème fraîche or sour cream. Ladle into warmed bowls, swirl a little of the remaining crème fraîche or sour cream on top of each and sprinkle with chives.

COOK'S TIP
Dried mushrooms have a rich, intense flavour and are perfect for boosting the flavour of cultivated mushrooms, which can often be rather bland.

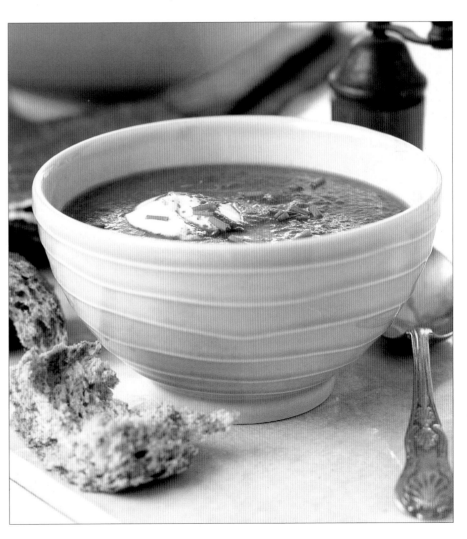

Nutritional information per portion: Energy 143Kcal/592kJ; Protein 3.7g; Carbohydrate 8.2g, of which sugars 3.2g; Fat 9g, of which saturates 5.3g; Cholesterol 22mg; Calcium 41mg; Fibre 2g; Sodium 174mg.

SEAFOOD CHOWDER

The word chowder takes its name from the French chaudière *– a pot traditionally used for making soups and stews. Like most chowders, this is a substantial dish, and could be served with crusty bread for a tasty lunch or supper.*

3 Sprinkle the flour over the leek mixture and stir in. Gradually add the remaining milk, stirring after each addition. Stir in the stock, followed by the corn mixture. Cover the slow cooker with the lid and cook for 2 hours.

4 Add the rice to the pot and cook for 30 minutes. Meanwhile, pull the corals away from the scallops and slice the white flesh into 5mm/¼in slices. Cut the fish fillet into bitesize chunks.

5 Add the scallops and fish to the chowder and gently stir to combine. Cover and cook for 15 minutes.

6 Stir the corals, parsley and cayenne pepper into the chowder and cook for 5–10 minutes, or until the vegetables, rice and fish are cooked through. Stir in the cream, if using, ladle into bowls, sprinkle with a little chopped parsley and serve immediately.

SERVES 4

25g/1oz/2 tbsp butter
1 small leek, sliced
1 small garlic clove, crushed
1 celery stalk, chopped
2 rindless smoked streaky (fatty) bacon
   rashers (strips), finely chopped
200g/7oz/generous 1 cup drained, canned
   corn kernels
450ml/¾ pint/scant 2 cups milk
5ml/1 tsp plain (all-purpose) flour
450ml/¾ pint/scant 2 cups boiling chicken
   or vegetable stock
115g/4oz/generous ½ cup easy-cook
   (converted) rice
4 large scallops, preferably with corals
115g/4oz white fish fillet, such as monkfish
15ml/1 tbsp chopped fresh parsley, plus
   extra to garnish
pinch of cayenne pepper
45ml/3 tbsp single (light) cream (optional)
salt and ground black pepper

1 Melt the butter in a frying pan, add the leek, garlic, celery and bacon and cook, stirring frequently, for 10 minutes, until soft but not browned. Transfer the mixture to the ceramic cooking pot and switch the slow cooker on to high.

2 Place half the corn kernels in a food processor or blender. Add about 75ml/2½fl oz/⅓ cup of the milk and process until the mixture is well blended and fairly thick and creamy.

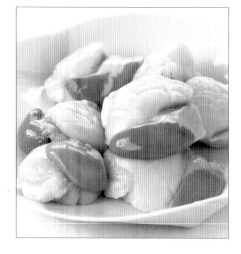

Nutritional information per portion: Energy 355Kcal/1497kJ; Protein 18.5g; Carbohydrate 45.9g, of which sugars 10.8g; Fat 12.1g, of which saturates 5.8g; Cholesterol 49mg; Calcium 179mg; Fibre 1.5g; Sodium 655mg.

AVGOLEMONO

This light, delicate soup is a great favourite in Greece and is a fine example of a few carefully chosen ingredients combining to make a delicious dish. It is essential to use a stock that is well flavoured, so use home-made if you can.

SERVES 4

900ml/1½ pints/3¾ cups near-boiling
   chicken stock
50g/2oz/⅓ cup easy-cook (converted)
   white rice
3 egg yolks
30–60ml/2–4 tbsp lemon juice
30ml/2 tbsp finely chopped fresh parsley
salt and ground black pepper
lemon slices and parsley sprigs, to garnish

1 Pour the stock into the ceramic cooking pot. Cover with a lid and cook on high for 30 minutes, or until it reaches boiling point.

2 Stir in the rice, cover and cook for 45 minutes, or until the rice is tender. Season to taste with salt and pepper. Switch off the slow cooker, remove the lid and leave to stand for 5 minutes.

3 Meanwhile, whisk the egg yolks in a bowl, then add about 30ml/2 tbsp of the lemon juice, whisking constantly until the mixture is smooth and bubbly. Add a ladleful of the hot soup to the egg mixture, whisking continuously.

4 Slowly add the egg mixture to the soup in the ceramic cooking pot, whisking all the time. The soup will thicken slightly and turn a pretty yellow.

5 Taste and add more lemon juice and seasoning if necessary. Stir in the parsley and serve immediately, garnished with lemon slices and parsley sprigs.

COOK'S TIP
When adding the egg mixture, you need to be careful not to let the soup curdle. You should avoid whisking the mixture into boiling liquid, so allow the soup to cool very slightly before whisking in the egg mixture in a slow, steady stream. Do not reheat the soup.

Nutritional information per portion: Energy 98Kcal/410kJ; Protein 3.3g; Carbohydrate 11.1g, of which sugars 0.3g; Fat 4.8g, of which saturates 1.3g; Cholesterol 151mg; Calcium 26mg; Fibre 0.1g; Sodium 211mg.

SPICED CARROT DIP

When carrots are cooked over a slow, gentle heat, their flavour intensifies and becomes deliciously sweet, making them the perfect partner for hot, spicy flavourings. Serve this tasty dip with wheat crackers or fiery tortilla chips.

SERVES 4

1 onion
3 carrots, plus extra grated carrot
    to garnish (optional)
grated rind and juice of 1 orange
15ml/1 tbsp hot curry paste
150ml/¼ pint/⅔ cup plain yogurt
handful of fresh basil leaves
15ml/1 tbsp fresh lemon juice
dash Tabasco sauce (optional)
salt and ground black pepper

1 Chop the onion very finely. Peel and grate the carrots. Put the onion, carrots, orange rind and juice, and curry paste in the ceramic cooking pot and stir well to combine. Cover with the lid and cook on high for 2 hours, or until the carrots are soft and tender.

2 Uncover the pot and leave to cool for about 10 minutes, then tip the mixture into a food processor or blender and process until smooth.

3 Transfer the carrot purée to a mixing bowl and leave, uncovered, for about 1 hour to cool completely.

4 Add the yogurt to the cooled carrot purée. Tear the basil leaves roughly into small pieces, then stir them into the mixture until thoroughly combined.

5 Stir in the lemon juice and Tabasco, if using, then season to taste with salt and pepper. Serve at room temperature, within a few hours of making.

Nutritional information per portion: Energy 58Kcal/241kJ; Protein 2.5g; Carbohydrate 9.5g, of which sugars 8.4g; Fat 1.3g, of which saturates 0.4g; Cholesterol 0mg; Calcium 80mg; Fibre 1.3g; Sodium 34mg.

CHEESE-STUFFED PEARS

These pears, with their scrumptious creamy topping, make a sublime dish when served with a simple salad. If you don't have a very large slow cooker, choose short squat pears rather than long, tapering ones, so that they will fit in a single layer.

SERVES 4

50g/2oz/¼ cup ricotta cheese
50g/2oz/¼ cup dolcelatte cheese
15ml/1 tbsp honey
½ celery stick, finely sliced
8 green olives, pitted and
   roughly chopped
4 dates, stoned (pitted) and cut into
   thin strips
pinch of paprika
2 medium barely ripe pears
150ml/¼ pint/⅔ cup apple juice
salad leaves, to serve (optional)

1 Place the ricotta cheese in a bowl and crumble in the dolcelatte. Add the honey, celery, olives, dates and paprika and mix together well until creamy and thoroughly blended.

2 Halve the pears lengthways. Use a melon baller or teaspoon to remove the cores and make a hollow for the filling.

3 Divide the ricotta filling equally between the pears, packing it into the hollow, then arrange the fruit in a single layer in the ceramic cooking pot.

4 Pour the apple juice around the pears, then cover with the lid. Cook on high for 1½–2 hours, or until the fruit is tender. (The cooking time will depend on the ripeness of the pears.)

5 Remove the pears from the slow cooker. If you like, brown them under a hot grill (broiler) for a few minutes. Serve with salad leaves, if you like.

COOK'S TIP
These pears go particularly well with slightly bitter and peppery leaves, such as chicory and rocket. Try them tossed in a walnut oil dressing.

Nutritional information per portion: Energy 236Kcal/992kJ; Protein 6.9g; Carbohydrate 35.6g, of which sugars 35.6g; Fat 8.2g, of which saturates 5.0g; Cholesterol 24mg; Calcium 141mg; Fibre 4.1g; Sodium 261mg.

COUNTRY-STYLE TERRINE with LEEKS

Traditionally, this sort of French pork terrine contains pork liver and egg to bind the mixture together. This version uses leeks instead to give a lighter result. In France, cornichons (small dill pickles or gherkins) and mustard are served as accompaniments.

3 Reserve two of the bacon rashers (strips) for the garnish, then finely chop the remaining bacon. Add to the pork mixture along with the leeks, herbs, spices, salt and pepper. Mix together, using a wooden spoon or your fingertips, until thoroughly combined.

4 Lightly grease the base and sides of a 1.2 litre/2 pint/5 cup heatproof dish or loaf tin (pan) with oil and line with greaseproof (waxed) paper. Put an upturned saucer or metal pastry ring in the base of the ceramic cooking pot and pour in 2.5cm/1in of hot water. Turn the slow cooker to high.

SERVES 8

350g/12oz trimmed leeks
25g/1oz/2 tbsp butter
2 garlic cloves, finely chopped
900g/2lb lean pork leg or shoulder
115g/4oz rinded smoked streaky
   (fatty) bacon
5ml/1 tsp chopped fresh thyme
3 sage leaves, finely chopped
1.5ml/¼ tsp quatre épices (see Cook's Tip)
1.5ml/¼ tsp ground cumin
2.5ml/½ tsp salt
2.5ml/½ tsp ground black pepper
3 bay leaves

COOK'S TIP
Quatre épices is a classic French spice mix containing ground cloves, cinnamon, nutmeg and pepper.

1 Cut the leeks lengthways, wash well and slice thinly. Melt the butter in a large heavy pan, add the leeks, then cover and cook over medium-low heat for about 10 minutes, stirring occasionally. Add the garlic and continue cooking for a further 10 minutes until the leeks are very soft. Set aside to cool.

2 Trim off any excess fat and gristle from the pork, then cut the meat into 2.5cm/1in cubes. Working in two or three batches, put the meat into a food processor fitted with a metal blade; the bowl should be about half-full. Pulse to chop the meat to a coarse purée. Alternatively, pass the meat through the coarse blade of a meat grinder. Transfer the meat to a large mixing bowl and remove any white stringy pieces.

5 Spoon the meat mixture into the prepared dish or tin, pressing it into the corners. Tap firmly to settle the mixture, and smooth the top. Arrange the bay leaves and reserved bacon (trimmed to size) on top, then cover with foil.

6 Place the dish or tin in the slow cooker and pour in enough boiling water to come just over halfway up the sides. Cover with the lid and cook for 4–5 hours or until cooked; the juices of the pâté should run clear when pierced with a skewer. Lift out of the ceramic cooking pot and leave to cool in the dish or tin.

7 Put the dish or tin on a tray, then place a foil-covered plate or board (just smaller than the size of the dish or tin) on top of the pâté. Weight the plate or board with two or three large cans or other heavy objects, and chill for several hours, or preferably overnight.

Nutritional information per portion: Energy 211Kcal/884kJ; Protein 27.5g; Carbohydrate 1.3g, of which sugars 1g; Fat 10.7g, of which saturates 4.4g; Cholesterol 87mg; Calcium 20mg; Fibre 1.0g; Sodium 395mg.

FISH TERRINE

This colourful layered terrine makes a spectacular appetizer or main course on a special occasion. It is particularly good for entertaining because it can be made in advance, chilled until ready to serve, then arranged on plates at the last minute.

SERVES 6

450g/1lb skinless white fish fillets
225g/8oz thinly sliced smoked salmon
2 egg whites, chilled
1.5ml/¼ tsp each salt and ground
    white pepper
pinch of freshly grated nutmeg
250ml/8fl oz/1 cup double (heavy) cream
50g/2oz small tender fresh spinach leaves
lemon mayonnaise, to serve

1 Cut the white fish fillets into 2.5cm/1in pieces, removing any bones. Spread out the fish pieces on a plate, cover with clear film (plastic wrap) and chill in the freezer for 15 minutes until very cold.

2 Lightly oil a 1.2 litre/2 pint/5 cup terrine or loaf tin (pan). Line the base and sides of the tin with the smoked salmon slices, making sure they overlap each other all the way around and letting them hang over the edges of the tin.

3 Remove the white fish from the freezer, then place in a food processor and blend to make a very smooth purée. (You may need to stop the machine and scrape down the sides two or three times as you do this.)

4 Add the egg whites, one at a time, processing after each addition, then add the salt, pepper and nutmeg. With the machine running, pour in the cream and stop as soon as it is blended. (If over-processed the cream will thicken.)

5 Transfer the fish mixture to a large glass bowl. Put the spinach leaves into the food processor and process to make a smooth purée. Add one-third of the fish mixture to the spinach and process briefly until just combined, scraping down the sides once or twice.

6 Pour about 2.5cm/1in of very hot water into the ceramic cooking pot. Place an upturned saucer or metal pastry ring in the base, then turn the slow cooker on to high.

7 Spread half the plain fish mixture in the base of the tin. Spoon the green fish mixture over the top and smooth it level, then cover with the remaining plain mixture. Fold the overhanging pieces of smoked salmon over the top to enclose the mixture. Tap the tin to settle the mixture and remove any air pockets, then cover the tin with a double layer of lightly oiled foil.

8 Put the tin in the slow cooker and pour in enough boiling water to come just over halfway up the sides. Cook for 3–3½ hours, or until a skewer inserted into the terrine comes out clean. Leave the terrine to cool in the tin, then chill in the refrigerator until firm.

9 To serve the terrine, turn out on to a board, remove the lining paper and slice. Arrange the slices on individual plates and serve with lemon mayonnaise.

Nutritional information per portion: Energy 340Kcal/1409kJ; Protein 23.2g; Carbohydrate 0.8g, of which sugars 0.8g; Fat 27.1g, of which saturates 14.7g; Cholesterol 110mg; Calcium 50mg; Fibre 0.2g; Sodium 201mg.

FISH AND SHELLFISH

Delicious, healthy and perfectly suited to cooking in a slow cooker, fish and shellfish can be used in a fabulous range of dishes. The gentle heat of this method cooks the delicate flesh to perfection every time. Although large whole fish, such as salmon, are too big for the slow cooker, smaller fish, such as herring and red mullet, and fish steaks, fillets and shellfish are perfect. Unlike meat, fish cooks relatively quickly in the slow cooker, so is ideal for combining with rice or pasta. It is incredibly versatile and can be cooked in all kinds of ways, to make both light and hearty dishes. Try salmon risotto with cucumber for a light and sophisticated summer dish, or hoki balls in tomato sauce for a satisfying family meal.

CREAMY ANCHOVY and POTATO BAKE

This classic Scandinavian dish of potatoes, onions and anchovies cooked with cream makes a hearty winter lunch or simple supper, served with a refreshing salad. In Norway and Sweden, it is often served as a hot appetizer.

2 Use half of the butter to grease the base and sides of the ceramic cooking pot, and layer half the potatoes and onions in the base of the dish.

3 Drain the anchovies, reserving 15ml/ 1 tbsp of the oil. Cut the anchovies into thin strips and lay these over the potatoes and onions, then layer the remaining potatoes and onions on top.

4 Combine the single cream and anchovy oil in a small jug (pitcher) and season with a little ground black pepper. Pour the mixture evenly over the potatoes and dot the surface with butter.

5 Cover and cook on high for 3½ hours, or until the potatoes and onions are tender. Brown under a hot grill (broiler), if you like, then drizzle over the double cream and sprinkle with parsley and pepper. Serve with fresh crusty bread.

SERVES 4

1kg/2¼ lb maincrop potatoes
2 onions
25g/1oz/2 tbsp butter
2 x 50g/2oz cans anchovy fillets
150ml/¼ pint/⅔ cup single (light) cream
150ml/¼ pint/⅔ cup double (heavy) cream
15ml/1 tbsp chopped fresh parsley
ground black pepper
fresh crusty bread, to serve

COOK'S TIP

This recipe can also be served as an appetizer for six, or as a side dish to accompany a main meal.

1 Peel the potatoes and cut into slices slightly thicker than 1cm/½in. Cut the slices into strips slightly more than 1cm/½in wide. Peel the onions and cut into very thin rings.

Nutritional information per portion: Energy 378Kcal/1580kJ; Protein 11.3g; Carbohydrate 37.9g, of which sugars 6.4g; Fat 21.2g, of which saturates 11.4g; Cholesterol 54mg; Calcium 1460mg; Fibre 11.5g; Sodium 133mg.

SALMON RISOTTO with CUCUMBER

A classic risotto is time-consuming to make because the stock needs to be added very gradually and requires constant attention from the cook. Here, the wine and stock are added in one go, making it far easier, yet still giving a delicious, creamy texture.

SERVES 4

25g/1oz/2 tbsp butter
small bunch of spring onions (scallions),
    finely sliced
½ cucumber, peeled, seeded
    and chopped
225g/8oz/generous 1 cup easy-cook
    (converted) Italian rice
750ml/1¼ pints/3 cups boiling vegetable
    or fish stock
120ml/4fl oz/½ cup white wine
450g/1lb salmon fillet, skinned
    and diced
45ml/3 tbsp chopped fresh tarragon
salt and ground black pepper

1 Put the butter in the ceramic cooking pot and switch the slow cooker to high. Leave to melt for 15 minutes, then stir in the spring onions and cucumber. Cover and cook for 30 minutes.

2 Add the rice to the pot and stir, then pour in the stock and wine. Cover with the lid and cook for 45 minutes, stirring once halfway through cooking.

3 Stir the diced salmon into the risotto and season with salt and pepper. Cook for a further 15 minutes, or until the rice is tender and the salmon just cooked. Switch off the slow cooker and leave the risotto to stand for 5 minutes.

4 Remove the lid, add the chopped tarragon and mix lightly. Spoon the risotto into individual warmed serving bowls or plates and serve immediately.

COOK'S TIP
Frozen peas can be used instead of cucumber, if you like. These should be defrosted and stirred into the risotto at the same time as the salmon.

Nutritional information per portion: Energy 506Kcal/2122kJ; Protein 28.4g; Carbohydrate 51.3g, of which sugars 2.8g; Fat 20g, of which saturates 5.9g; Cholesterol 70mg; Calcium 91mg; Fibre 1.4g; Sodium 266mg.

MIXED FISH JAMBALAYA

As with the Spanish paella, the ingredients used to make this classic Creole dish can be varied according to what is available. The name jambalaya is thought to have come from the French word for ham – jambon – and the Creole word for rice – à la ya.

SERVES 4

30ml/2 tbsp oil
6 rashers (strips) rinded smoked streaky (fatty) bacon, chopped
1 onion, chopped
2 sticks celery, sliced
2 garlic cloves, crushed
5ml/1 tsp cayenne pepper
2 bay leaves
5ml/1 tsp dried oregano
2.5ml/½ tsp dried thyme
4 tomatoes, skinned, seeded and chopped
750ml/1¼ pints/3 cups boiling vegetable or fish stock
15ml/1 tbsp tomato purée (paste)
300g/10oz/1½ cups easy-cook (converted) rice
225g/8oz firm white fish, such as haddock, skinned, boned and cubed
115g/4oz cooked prawns (shrimp)
salt and ground black pepper
4 spring onions (scallions) and 4 cooked prawns (shrimp) in their shells, to garnish

1 Heat the oil in a frying pan and cook the bacon over a medium-high heat for 2 minutes. Reduce the heat, add the onion and celery and cook for a further 5–10 minutes, or until soft and beginning to turn brown.

2 Transfer the mixture to the ceramic cooking pot and switch the slow cooker to high. Add the garlic, cayenne pepper, bay leaves, oregano, thyme, tomatoes, boiling stock and tomato purée. Stir well to mix, then cover with the lid and cook for about 1 hour.

3 Sprinkle the rice over the tomato mixture, followed by the cubes of fish. Season with salt and pepper and stir. Re-cover and cook for 45 minutes.

4 Add the prawns and stir, then cook for 15 minutes, or until the fish and rice are tender and most of the liquid has been absorbed. Serve garnished with spring onions and prawns in their shells.

COOK'S TIP
If you like a really hot, spicy bite to your jambalaya, serve with a little hot chilli sauce for sprinkling over at the table.

Nutritional information per portion: Energy 243Kcal/1015kJ; Protein 23.2g; Carbohydrate 6.5g, of which sugars 5.4g; Fat 14g, of which saturates 3.4g; Cholesterol 126mg; Calcium 64mg; Fibre 1.6g; Sodium 1303mg.

HOKI BALLS in TOMATO SAUCE

This simple fish dish is ideal for serving to young children because there is no risk of bones. For adults, it can be spiced up with a dash of chilli sauce. It is low in fat and therefore ideal for anyone on a low-fat or low-cholesterol diet.

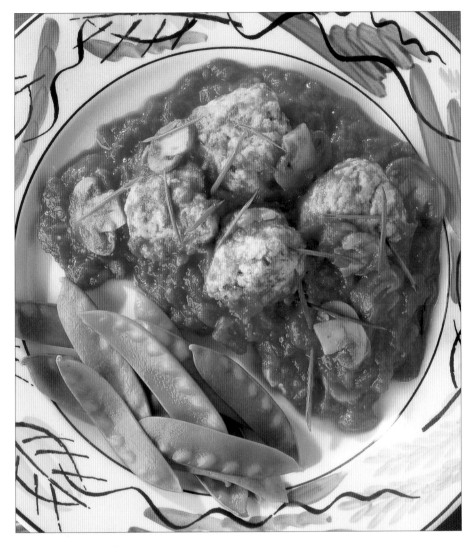

2 Meanwhile, cut the fish into large chunks and place in a food processor. Add the breadcrumbs and the chives or spring onions and season with salt and pepper. Process until the fish is finely chopped, but still has some texture.

3 Divide the mixture into 16 even-size pieces, then roll them into balls with damp hands. Put the fish balls on a plate and chill in the refrigerator until needed.

4 About 30 minutes before the end of the sauce's cooking time, take the fish balls out of the refrigerator and leave them to stand at room temperature.

5 Add the fishballs to the sauce in a single layer. Cook for 1 hour on high, then reduce the temperature to low and cook for a further hour, or until the fish balls are thoroughly cooked. Serve hot, garnished with chives and accompanied by steamed green vegetables.

SERVES 4

400g/14oz can chopped tomatoes
50g/2oz button mushrooms, sliced
450g/1lb hoki or other firm white fish
   fillets, skinned
15g/½oz/¼ cup wholemeal
   (whole-wheat) breadcrumbs
30ml/2 tbsp chopped fresh chives or
   spring onions (scallions)
salt and ground black pepper
chopped fresh chives, to garnish
steamed green vegetables, to serve

COOK'S TIP

If hoki is not available, you can use the same weight of cod, haddock or whiting.

1 Pour the chopped tomatoes into the ceramic cooking pot, then add the sliced mushrooms and a little salt and ground black pepper. Cover with the lid, switch the slow cooker to high and cook for about 2 hours.

Nutritional information per portion: Energy 116Kcal/490kJ; Protein 22.2g; Carbohydrate 4.6g, of which sugars 2.9g; Fat 1.0g, of which saturates 0.1g; Cholesterol 52mg; Calcium 27mg; Fibre 1.0g; Sodium 125mg.

SPINACH and NUT STUFFED HERRINGS

It is difficult to cook large whole fish in a slow cooker, but smaller fish, such as sardines and herrings, are ideal. Their slightly oily flesh is perfectly suited to slow cooking, too, because it helps to keep the fish wonderfully moist.

SERVES 4

40g/1½oz/3 tbsp unsalted (sweet) butter
5ml/1 tsp sunflower oil
25g/1oz/¼ cup pine nuts
1 small onion, finely chopped
175g/6oz frozen spinach, thawed
50g/2oz/1 cup white breadcrumbs
25g/1oz/⅓ cup grated Parmesan cheese
pinch of freshly grated nutmeg
75ml/5 tbsp fish or vegetable stock
    or white wine
4 small herrings, heads removed,
    and boned
salt and ground black pepper
lemon wedges, to serve

1 Heat 25g/1oz/2 tbsp of the butter and sunflower oil in a frying pan until melted. Add the pine nuts and gently fry for 3–4 minutes until golden. Lift them from the pan with a slotted spoon, leaving the fat behind, and place in a mixing bowl.

2 Add the finely chopped onion to the pan and cook gently for 10 minutes, stirring frequently, until soft.

3 Meanwhile, place the thawed spinach in a fine sieve (strainer) and press out as much liquid as possible. (Use your hands to squeeze out the liquid, or press firmly with the back of a spoon.)

4 Put the onion and spinach in the mixing bowl with the pine nuts and add the breadcrumbs, cheese, nutmeg, salt and pepper. Mix the ingredients with a fork until thoroughly combined.

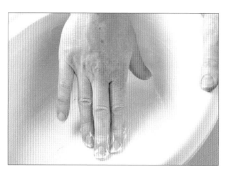

5 Smear the remaining 15g/½oz/1 tbsp of butter over the base of the ceramic cooking pot and pour in the stock or wine. Cover with the lid and switch the slow cooker on to high.

6 Using a sharp knife, make three shallow cuts down each side of the fish, then spoon the stuffing into the cavities, packing it in quite firmly. Bring the edges of the fish together and secure with wooden cocktail sticks (toothpicks).

7 Arrange the fish on the base of the ceramic cooking pot in a single layer. Cover the pot with the lid and cook for 1½–2½ hours, or until the fish is cooked. (Test the flesh with a fork; it should flake easily when ready.)

8 Carefully lift the stuffed fish out of the slow cooker on to warmed serving plates, and serve with lemon wedges.

COOK'S TIP
This dish is perfect for a simple, tasty supper, but it is great for entertaining, too. Serve with a tasty couscous salad tossed with plenty of herbs and raisins. The sweetness of the dried fruit goes particularly well with the spinach and pine nut stuffing, and complements the rich flavour of the fish.

VARIATIONS
• Other kinds of nuts can be used in place of pine nuts in the stuffing. Try chopped hazelnuts or walnuts instead.
• As an alternative to nuts, add 15ml/1 tbsp chopped dried apricots to the stuffing.

Nutritional information per portion: Energy 351Kcal/1462kJ; Protein 24g; Carbohydrate 7.6g, of which sugars 1.9g; Fat 23.9g, of which saturates 6.9g; Cholesterol 78mg; Calcium 619mg; Fibre 1.5g; Sodium 624mg.

POULTRY AND GAME

The slow cooker is perfect for making all kinds of stews, casseroles and curries, and this chapter is packed with fantastic, healthy recipe ideas using poultry and game as the basis. Chicken is always a firm favourite, and the versatility of the slow cooker guarantees that there is something here for everyone. There are also other poultry and game dishes to whet the appetite, using turkey, guinea fowl and hare. All of these recipes are wonderfully tasty and are destined to become firm family favourites. Try Jamaican Jerk chicken, Turkey and Tomato Hot Pot, Guinea Fowl and Spring Vegetable Stew or Hare Pot Pies.

TURKEY and TOMATO HOT-POT

Often reserved for festive meals, turkey makes a great choice for any occasion. Here the meat is shaped into balls and simmered with rice in a richly flavoured tomato sauce.

SERVES 4

white bread loaf, unsliced
30ml/2 tbsp milk
1 garlic clove, crushed
2.5ml/½ tsp caraway seeds
225g/8oz minced (ground) turkey
1 egg white
350ml/12fl oz/1½ cups near-boiling
   chicken stock
400g/14oz can chopped tomatoes
15ml/1 tbsp tomato purée (paste)
90g/3½oz/½ cup easy-cook
   (converted) rice
salt and ground black pepper
15ml/1 tbsp chopped fresh basil, to garnish
courgette (zucchini) ribbons, to serve

1 Using a serrated knife, remove the crusts and cut the bread into cubes.

2 Place the bread in a mixing bowl and sprinkle with the milk, then leave to soak for about 5 minutes.

3 Add the garlic clove, caraway seeds, turkey, and salt and pepper to the bread and mix together well.

4 Whisk the egg white until stiff, then fold, half at a time, into the turkey mixture. Chill in the refrigerator.

5 Pour the stock into the ceramic cooking pot. Add the tomatoes and tomato purée, then switch to high, cover with the lid and cook for 1 hour.

6 Meanwhile, shape the turkey mixture into 16 small balls. Stir the rice into the tomato mixture, then add the turkey balls. Cook on high for a further hour, or until the turkey balls and rice are cooked. Serve with the courgettes.

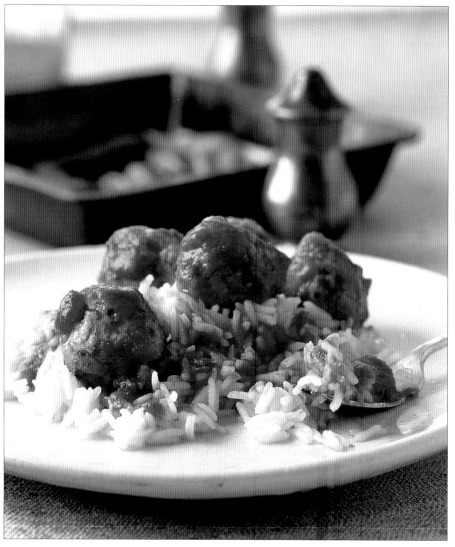

Nutritional information per portion: Energy 187Kcal/797kJ; Protein 18.2g; Carbohydrate 26.6g, of which sugars 3.9g; Fat 1.7g, of which saturates 0.5g; Cholesterol 32mg; Calcium 44mg; Fibre 1g; Sodium 212mg.

LAYERED CHICKEN and MUSHROOM BAKE

*This rich, creamy dish makes a hearty winter supper. The thick sauce combines with
juices from the mushrooms and chicken during cooking to make a well-flavoured gravy.*

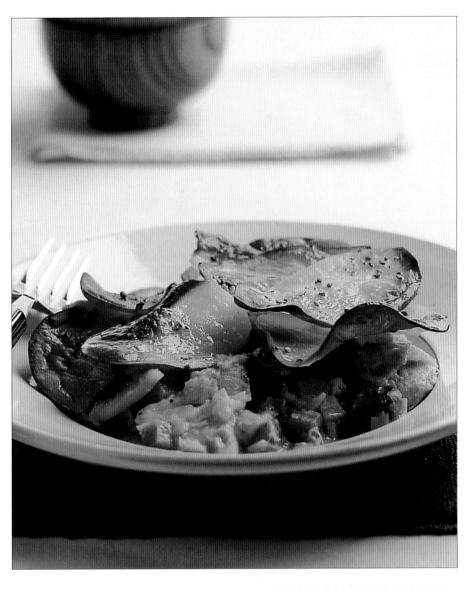

2 Add 25g/1oz/2 tbsp of the butter to the pan and heat gently until melted. Stir in the leek and fry gently for about minutes. Sprinkle the flour over the leeks, then turn off the heat and gradually blend in the milk until smooth. Slowly bring the mixture to the boil, stirring all the time, until thickened.

3 Remove the pan from the heat and stir in the Worcestershire sauce, if using, mustard, diced carrot, mushrooms and chicken. Season generously.

4 Arrange enough potato slices to cover the base of the ceramic cooking pot. Spoon one-third of the chicken mixture over the top, then cover with another layer of potatoes. Repeat layering, finishing with a layer of potatoes. Dot the remaining butter on top.

5 Cover and cook on high for 4 hours, or until the potatoes are cooked and tender when pierced with a skewer. If you like, place the dish under a moderate grill (broiler) for 5 minutes to brown, then serve.

SERVES 4

15ml/1 tbsp olive oil
4 large chicken breast portions,
   cut into chunks
40g/1½oz/3 tbsp butter
1 leek, finely sliced into rings
25g/1oz/¼ cup plain (all-purpose) flour
550ml/18fl oz/2½ cups milk
5ml/1 tsp Worcestershire sauce (optional)
5ml/1 tsp wholegrain mustard
1 carrot, finely diced
225g/8oz/3 cups button (white)
   mushrooms, thinly sliced
900g/2lb potatoes, thinly sliced
salt and ground black pepper

1 Heat the olive oil in a large pan. Add the chicken and fry gently until beginning to brown. Remove the chicken from the pan using a slotted spoon, leaving any juices behind. Set aside.

Nutritional information per portion: Energy 461Kcal/1943kJ; Protein 42.4g; Carbohydrate 43.8g, of which sugars 5.2g; Fat 14.1g, of which saturates 6.4g; Cholesterol 126.3mg; Calcium 49mg; Fibre 4.3g; Sodium 351mg.

SPRING CHICKEN SLOW-BRAISED in SMOKY BACON SAUCE

Sweet, succulent and tangy with the flavour of apples and aromatic thyme, this delicious stew makes a great alternative to the classic roast. Baby spring chickens are also known as poussin and can weigh 350–500g/12oz–1¼lb. Be sure to buy large ones because the smaller birds are only big enough for a single serving.

SERVES 4

2 large spring chickens
25g/1oz/2 tbsp unsalted
   (sweet) butter
10ml/2 tsp sunflower oil
115g/4oz chopped bacon pieces
   or smoked streaky (fatty) bacon
2 leeks, washed and sliced
175g/6oz/2¼ cup small button (white)
   mushrooms, trimmed
120ml/4fl oz/½ cup apple juice,
   plus a further 15ml/1 tbsp
120ml/4fl oz/½ cup chicken stock
30ml/2 tbsp clear honey
10ml/2 tsp chopped fresh thyme
   or 2.5ml/½ tsp dried
225g/8oz crisp red apples
10ml/2 tsp cornflour (cornstarch)
salt and ground black pepper
creamy mashed potatoes and
   pan-fried or steamed baby leeks,
   to serve

1 Using a sharp, heavy knife or a meat cleaver, carefully split the spring chickens in half to make four portions. Rinse the portions well under cold running water, then pat dry using kitchen paper.

2 Heat the butter and sunflower oil in a large pan and add the spring chicken portions. Fry, turning the pieces over, until lightly browned on all sides. Transfer the chicken portions to the ceramic cooking pot, leaving the cooking fat in the pan.

3 Add the chopped bacon to the pan and cook for about 5 minutes, stirring occasionally, until beginning to brown.

4 Using a slotted spoon transfer the bacon to the ceramic cooking pot, leaving all the fat and juices behind.

5 Add the leeks and mushrooms to the pan and cook for a few minutes until they begin to soften and the mushrooms begin to release their juices.

6 Pour 120ml/4fl oz/½ cup apple juice and the chicken stock into the pan, then stir in the honey and thyme. Season well with salt and ground black pepper.

7 Bring the mixture almost to boiling point, then pour over the chicken and bacon. Cover the ceramic cooking pot with the lid, switch the slow cooker to high and cook for 2 hours.

8 Quarter, core and thickly slice the apples. Add them to the cooking pot, submerging them in the liquid to stop them turning brown. Cook for a further 2 hours, or until the chicken and vegetables are cooked and tender.

9 Remove the chicken from the cooking pot, place on a plate and keep warm.

10 Blend the cornflour with the 15ml/1 tbsp apple juice and stir into the cooking liquid until thickened. Taste and adjust the seasoning, if necessary.

11 Serve the chicken on warmed plates with sauce poured over the top. Accompany with mashed potatoes and pan-fried or steamed baby leeks.

COOK'S TIP
Always check that chicken is thoroughly cooked before serving to avoid any risk of salmonella. To test, pierce the thickest part of the meat with a skewer or thin knife; the juices should run clear.

Nutritional information per portion: Energy 465Kcal/1945kJ; Protein 32.8g; Carbohydrate 25.9g, of which sugars 20.7g; Fat 26.3g, of which saturates 9.5g; Cholesterol 172mg; Calcium 40mg; Fibre 3.3g; Sodium 632mg.

HEN in a POT with PARSLEY SAUCE

Although harder to find nowadays, a boiling fowl will feed a family well. A large chicken could replace the boiling fowl. Serve with potatoes boiled in their jackets and cabbage.

SERVES 6

1.6–1.8kg/3½–4lb boiling fowl or
   whole chicken
½ lemon, sliced
small bunch of parsley and thyme
675g/1½lb carrots, cut into large chunks
12 shallots or small onions, left whole

For the sauce
50g/2oz/½ cup butter
50g/2oz/½ cup plain (all-purpose) flour
15ml/1 tbsp lemon juice
60ml/4 tbsp chopped flat leaf parsley
150ml/½ pint/⅔ cup milk
salt and ground black pepper
sprigs of flat leaf parsley, to garnish

VARIATION
A small joint of ham or bacon can also be added to the pot if available. Soak it overnight in cold water before cooking and do not add any extra salt without tasting first. A boiling fowl with a small joint of bacon, weighing 900g–1kg/2–2¼lb in total, should feed 8–10 people. Red cabbage makes a tasty accompaniment.

1 Remove any trussing string and loose pieces of fat from inside the boiling fowl or chicken, then rinse under cold water and place in the ceramic cooking pot. Add the lemon, parsley and thyme, carrots and onions and season well.

2 Pour in near-boiling water to just cover the fowl and vegetables. Cover with the lid, switch the slow cooker to high and cook for 1 hour.

3 Skim off any scum and fat using a slotted spoon. Re-cover the pot and cook for 2–2½ hours, or until the fowl is cooked and tender. Using a slotted spoon, lift the fowl on to a warmed serving dish, arrange the vegetables around it and keep warm.

4 Strain the cooking liquid into a pan and boil uncovered to reduce by a third. Strain and leave to settle for 2 minutes, then skim the fat off the surface.

5 Melt the butter in a saucepan, add the flour and cook, stirring, for 1 minute. Gradually stir in the stock (there should be about 600ml/1 pint/2½ cups) and bring to the boil.

6 Add the lemon juice, parsley and milk to the pan. Season with salt and ground black pepper and simmer the sauce for another 1–2 minutes.

7 To serve, pour a little of the sauce over the fowl and add the carrots and onions, then garnish with a few sprigs of fresh parsley, and take to the table for carving. Pour the rest of the sauce into a warmed sauceboat and serve separately.

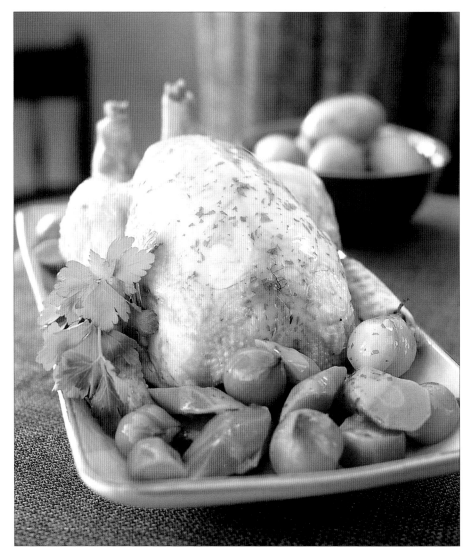

Nutritional information per portion: Energy 509Kcal/2114kJ; Protein 36.2g; Carbohydrate 20.1g, of which sugars 12.2g; Fat 32g, of which saturates 11.4g; Cholesterol 195mg; Calcium 109mg; Fibre 4g; Sodium 214mg

CHICKEN and SPLIT PEA STEW

*A traditional Persian Koresh – a thick saucy stew served with rice – is usually made
with lamb, but here chicken is used to create a lighter, lower-fat dish.*

SERVES 4

50g/2oz/¼ cup green split peas
45ml/3 tbsp olive oil
1 large onion, finely chopped
450g/1lb boneless chicken thighs
350ml/12fl oz/1½ cups boiling
   chicken stock
5ml/1 tsp ground turmeric
2.5ml/½ tsp ground cinnamon
1.5ml/¼ tsp grated nutmeg
30ml/2 tbsp dried mint
2 aubergines (eggplant), diced
8 ripe tomatoes, diced
2 garlic cloves, crushed
salt and ground black pepper
fresh mint, to garnish
plain boiled rice, to serve

1 Put the split peas in a large bowl. Pour in cold water to cover and leave to soak for at least 6 hours or overnight.

2 Tip the split peas into a sieve (strainer) and drain well. Place in a large pan, cover with fresh cold water and bring to the boil. Boil rapidly for 10 minutes, then rinse, drain and set aside.

3 Heat 15ml/1 tbsp of the oil in a pan, add the onion and cook for about 5 minutes. Add the chicken and cook until golden on all sides, then transfer to the ceramic cooking pot. Add the split peas, hot chicken stock, turmeric, cinnamon, nutmeg and mint and season well with salt and black pepper.

4 Cover the pot with the lid and cook on high or auto for 1 hour. Switch the slow cooker to low or leave on auto and cook for a further 3 hours, or until the chicken is just cooked and the split peas are nearly tender.

5 Heat the remaining 30ml/2 tbsp of oil in a frying pan, add the diced aubergines and cook for about 5 minutes until lightly browned. Add the tomatoes and garlic and cook for a further 2 minutes.

6 Transfer the aubergines to the ceramic cooking pot, stir to combine, then cook for about 1 hour. Sprinkle with fresh mint leaves to garnish and serve with plain boiled rice.

Nutritional information per portion: Energy 298Kcal/1251kJ; Protein 29.1g; Carbohydrate 18.5g, of which sugars 10.2g; Fat 12.5g, of which saturates 2.3g; Cholesterol 118mg; Calcium 48mg; Fibre 4.5g; Sodium 206mg.

CARIBBEAN PEANUT CHICKEN

Peanut butter adds a delicious richness and depth of flavour to this spicy rice dish.
It is a classic ingredient used in many slow-cooked Caribbean curries and stews.

3 Meanwhile, heat the remaining oil in a frying pan, add the onion and fry for 10 minutes until soft. Transfer to the ceramic cooking pot and switch the slow cooker to high. Add the chopped tomatoes and chilli and stir to combine.

4 Put the peanut butter into a bowl, then blend in the stock, adding a little at a time. Pour the mixture into the ceramic cooking pot, season and stir. Cover with the lid and cook for 1 hour.

5 About 30 minutes before the end of cooking time, remove the chicken from the refrigerator and leave it to come to room temperature.

6 Add the chicken and the marinade to the ceramic cooking pot and stir to mix. Re-cover and cook for 1 hour.

7 Sprinkle the rice over the casserole, then stir to mix. Cover and cook for a final 45 minutes–1 hour, or until the chicken and rice are cooked and tender. Serve straight away, garnished with lemon or lime wedges for squeezing over, and sprigs of fresh parsley.

SERVES 4

4 skinless, boneless chicken
   breast portions
45ml/3 tbsp groundnut (peanut) or
   sunflower oil
1 garlic clove, crushed
5ml/1 tsp chopped fresh thyme
15ml/1 tbsp curry powder
juice of half a lemon
1 onion, finely chopped
2 tomatoes, peeled, seeded and chopped
1 fresh green chilli, seeded and sliced
60ml/4 tbsp smooth peanut butter
750ml/1¼ pints/3 cups boiling
   chicken stock
300g/10oz/1½ cups easy-cook (converted)
   white rice
salt and ground black pepper
lemon or lime wedges and sprigs of fresh
   flat leaf parsley, to garnish

1 Cut the chicken breast portions into thin strips. In a bowl, mix together 15ml/1 tbsp of the oil with the garlic, thyme, curry powder and lemon juice.

2 Add the chicken strips to the ingredients in the bowl and stir well to combine. Cover with clear film (plastic wrap) and leave to marinate in the refrigerator for 1½–2 hours.

Nutritional information per portion: Energy 635Kcal/2677kJ; Protein 45.8g; Carbohydrate 70.7g, of which sugars 4.4g; Fat 20.8g, of which saturates 4.1g; Cholesterol 105mg; Calcium 65mg; Fibre 2.1g; Sodium 354mg.

JAMAICAN JERK CHICKEN

The word "jerk" refers to the herb and spice seasoning traditionally used to marinate meat in Jamaica. It was originally used only for pork, but jerked chicken is just as good.

SERVES 4

8 chicken pieces, such as thighs and legs
15ml/1 tbsp sunflower oil
15g/½ oz/1 tbsp unsalted (sweet) butter

For the sauce
1 bunch of spring onions (scallions),
    trimmed and finely chopped
2 garlic cloves, crushed
1 hot red chilli pepper, halved, seeded
    and finely chopped
5ml/1 tsp ground allspice
2.5ml/½ tsp ground cinnamon
5ml/1 tsp dried thyme
1.5ml/¼ tsp freshly grated nutmeg
10ml/2 tsp demerara sugar
15ml/1 tbsp plain (all-purpose) flour
300ml/½ pint/1¼ cups chicken stock
15ml/1 tbsp red or white wine vinegar
15ml/1 tbsp lime juice
10ml/2 tsp tomato purée (paste)
salt and ground black pepper
salad leaves or rice, to serve

VARIATION
For jerked pork, sauté 4 pork loin steaks
(each about 90g/3½oz) in oil for 30 seconds
on each side. Make the jerk sauce as above,
using vegetable instead of chicken stock.
Cook in the same way as the chicken recipe
above, and serve with plain boiled rice and
chargrilled pineapple wedges.

1 Wipe the chicken pieces, then pat dry on kitchen paper. Heat the oil and butter in a frying pan until melted, then add the chicken, in batches if necessary, and cook until browned on all sides. Remove with a slotted spoon, leaving the fat in the pan, and transfer to the ceramic cooking pot. Switch the slow cooker to high.

2 Add the spring onions, garlic and chilli to the frying pan and cook gently for 4–5 minutes, or until softened, stirring frequently. Stir in the allspice, cinnamon, thyme, nutmeg and sugar. Sprinkle in the flour and stir to mix, then gradually add the chicken stock, stirring until the mixture bubbles and thickens. Remove the pan from the heat.

3 Stir the vinegar, lime juice, tomato purée and some salt and ground black pepper into the sauce. Pour over the chicken pieces, cover with a lid and cook on high for 3–4 hours, or until the chicken is cooked and very tender.

4 Remove the chicken from the sauce and place on a serving dish. Taste the sauce and adjust the seasoning, then serve separately, with salad leaves or rice as an accompaniment.

COOK'S TIP
There are many recipes for jerk seasoning, but all include chillies, allspice and thyme. The spicy sauce not only flavours the meat, it also tenderizes it.

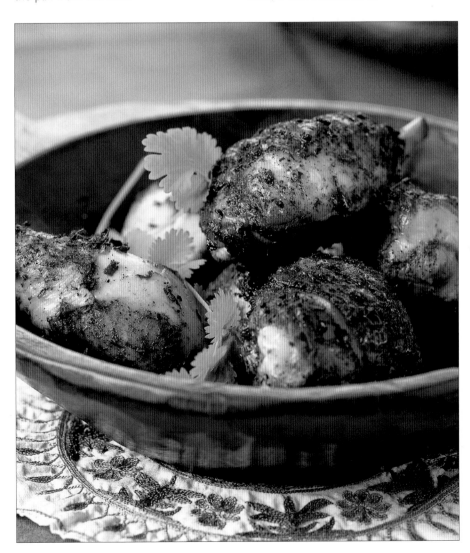

FRAGRANT CHICKEN CURRY

Lentils are used to thicken the sauce in this mild, fragrant curry, and fresh coriander gives the dish a really distinctive, fresh taste. The generous quantities of spinach mean that you won't need an additional vegetable dish to balance the meal.

2 Add the chicken to the lentil mixture, pressing it down in a single layer. Cover and cook on high for 3 hours, or until the chicken is just tender.

3 Add the spinach to the pot, pressing it down into the hot liquid. Cover and cook for a further 30 minutes until wilted. Stir in the chopped coriander.

4 Season the curry with salt and pepper to taste, then serve garnished with fresh coriander sprigs and accompanied with basmati rice and poppadums.

COOK'S TIP
You will need a large slow cooker to accomodate all the spinach in this recipe. It will shrink down during cooking, but the initial volume is large. If you have a small slow cooker, use thawed, well-drained frozen spinach instead.

SERVES 4

75g/3oz/scant ½ cup red lentils
30ml/2 tbsp mild curry powder
10ml/2 tsp ground coriander
5ml/1 tsp cumin seeds
350ml/12fl oz/1½ cups boiling vegetable
   or chicken stock
8 chicken thighs, skinned
225g/8oz fresh shredded spinach
15ml/1 tbsp chopped fresh
   coriander (cilantro)
salt and ground black pepper
sprigs of fresh coriander,
   to garnish
white or brown basmati rice
   and poppadums, to serve

1 Place the lentils in a sieve (strainer) and rinse under cold running water. Drain well, then put in the ceramic cooking pot with the curry powder, ground coriander, cumin seeds and stock. Cover and cook on high for 2 hours.

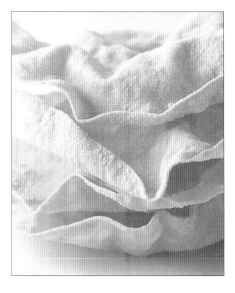

Nutritional information per portion: Energy 591Kcal/2490kJ; Protein 75.5g; Carbohydrate 38.2g, of which sugars 3.9g; Fat 16.1g, of which saturates 3.9g; Cholesterol 171mg; Calcium 426mg; Fibre 9.4g; Sodium 880mg.

CHICKEN in a CASHEW NUT SAUCE

*The Moguls had a profound impact on the Indian cuisine, and the resulting style
of cooking is known as Mughlai food. One of their legacies is the use of nut paste,
which is used here to give the curry a rich yet delicately flavoured sauce.*

SERVES 4

1 large onion, roughly chopped
1 clove garlic, crushed
15ml/1 tbsp tomato purée (paste)
50g/2oz/½ cup cashew nuts
7.5ml/1½ tsp garam masala
5ml/1 tsp chilli powder
1.5ml/¼ tsp ground turmeric
5ml/1 tsp salt
15ml/1 tbsp lemon juice
15ml/1 tbsp natural (plain) yogurt
30ml/2 tbsp vegetable oil
450g/1lb chicken breast fillets, skinned
    and cubed
175g/6oz/2¼ cups button (white)
    mushrooms
15ml/1 tbsp sultanas (golden raisins)
300ml/½ pint/1¼ cups chicken
    or vegetable stock
30ml/2 tbsp chopped fresh coriander
    (cilantro), plus extra to garnish
rice and fruit chutney, to serve

1 Put the onion, garlic, tomato purée,
cashew nuts, garam masala, chilli powder,
turmeric, salt, lemon juice and yogurt in
a food processor and process to a paste.

2 Heat the oil in a large frying pan or
wok and fry the cubes of chicken for a
few minutes, or until just beginning to
brown. Using a slotted spoon, transfer
the chicken to the ceramic cooking pot,
leaving the oil in the pan.

3 Add the spice paste and mushrooms
to the pan, lower the heat and fry gently,
stirring frequently, for 3–4 minutes. Tip
the mixture into the ceramic pot.

4 Add the sultanas to the pot and stir
in the chicken or vegetable stock. Cover
with the lid and switch the slow cooker
to high. Cook for 3–4 hours, stirring
halfway through the cooking time. The
chicken should be cooked through and
very tender, and the sauce fairly thick.

5 Stir the chopped coriander into the
sauce, then taste and add a little more
salt and pepper, if necessary. Serve the
curry from the ceramic cooking pot, or
transfer to a warmed serving dish, and
garnish with a sprinkling of chopped
fresh coriander. Serve with rice and a
fruit chutney, such as mango.

Nutritional information per portion: Energy 239Kcal/1006kJ; Protein 31.6g; Carbohydrate 10.7g, of which sugars 7.6g; Fat 8.1g, of which saturates 1.7g; Cholesterol 78.9mg; Calcium 39mg; Fibre 1.9g; Sodium 696mg.

GUINEA FOWL and SPRING VEGETABLE STEW

Resembling a well-flavoured chicken stew, this tasty dish of guinea fowl cooked with spring vegetables and flavoured with mustard and herbs is a sure winner.

SERVES 4

1.6kg/3½lb guinea fowl
45ml/3 tbsp plain (all-purpose) flour
45ml/3 tbsp olive oil
115g/4oz pancetta, cut into tiny cubes
1 onion, chopped
3 cloves garlic, chopped
200ml/7fl oz/scant 1 cup white wine
225g/8oz baby carrots
225g/8oz baby turnips
6 baby leeks, cut into 7.5cm/3in lengths
sprig of fresh thyme
1 bay leaf
10ml/2 tsp Dijon mustard
150ml/¼ pint/⅔ cup boiling chicken
   or vegetable stock
225g/8oz shelled peas
30ml/2 tbsp chopped fresh parsley
15ml/1 tbsp chopped fresh mint
salt and ground black pepper

1 Joint the guinea fowl into eight pieces. Wipe or lightly rinse them, then pat dry on kitchen paper. Season the flour with salt and pepper and toss the guinea fowl portions in it. Set aside any leftover flour.

2 Heat 30ml/2 tbsp of the oil in a large frying pan, add the pancetta and fry over a medium heat until lightly browned, stirring occasionally. Using a slotted spoon, transfer the pancetta to the ceramic cooking pot, leaving any fat and juices in the frying pan.

3 Add the guinea fowl portions to the pan and fry, turning, until browned on all sides. Arrange the guinea fowl portions in a single layer in the cooking pot on top of the pancetta.

4 Add the remaining 15ml/1 tbsp oil to the frying pan, add the onion and cook for 3–4 minutes, until just beginning to soften. Add the garlic and cook for about 1 minute, then stir in the reserved flour. Gradually stir in the wine and bring to the boil. Pour over the guinea fowl.

5 Add the carrots, turnips and leeks to the cooking pot with the thyme and bay leaf. Blend the mustard with the stock, season with salt and pepper and pour over. Cover with the lid and cook on high for 3–4 hours, or until the guinea fowl and vegetables are tender.

6 Add the peas to the stew and cook for a further 45 minutes. Taste and adjust the seasoning, then stir in most of the fresh herbs. Divide the stew among four warmed serving plates, sprinkle the remaining fresh herbs over the top and serve immediately.

COOK'S TIPS
• To save time on preparation, ask your butcher to joint the guinea fowl for you.
• Rabbit has a delicate flavour that goes well with the tender spring vegetables and herbs used in this stew. Try using eight rabbit joints in place of the guinea fowl.

Nutritional information per portion: Energy 581Kcal/2425kJ; Protein 50.5g; Carbohydrate 29.1g, of which sugars 11.2g; Fat 26.5g, of which saturates 7.4g; Cholesterol 224mg; Calcium 109mg; Fibre 6.9g; Sodium 668mg.

HARE POT PIES

The full, gamey flavour of hare is perfect for this dish, but boneless rabbit, venison, pheasant or any other game meat can be used instead. The meat filling is cooked in the slow cooker until tender and succulent – this can be done the day before if you like – before being topped with pastry and finished in the oven.

3 Heat the remaining oil in the pan and fry the hare in batches until well browned. When all the meat has been cooked, return it to the pan. Sprinkle over the flour and cook, stirring, for a few seconds, then gradually stir in the Madeira and stock and bring to the boil.

4 Transfer the hare mixture to the ceramic cooking pot and cook for 1 hour. Switch the slow cooker to low or leave on auto and cook for a further 5–6 hours, until the meat and vegetables are tender. Stir in the chopped parsley, then set aside to cool.

5 To make the pies, preheat the oven to 220°C/425°F/Gas 7. Spoon the hare mixture into four individual pie dishes. Cut the pastry into quarters and roll out on a lightly floured work surface to make the pie covers. Make the pieces larger than the dishes. Trim off any excess pastry and use the trimmings to line the rim of each dish.

6 Dampen the pastry rims with cold water and cover with the pastry lids. Pinch the edges together to seal in the filling. Brush each pie with beaten egg yolk and make a small hole in the top of each one to allow steam to escape.

7 Stand the pies on a baking tray and bake for 25 minutes, or until the pastry is well risen and dark golden. If the pastry is browning too quickly, cover with foil after 15 minutes to prevent it from overbrowning.

SERVES 4

45ml/3 tbsp olive oil
1 leek, sliced
225g/8oz parsnips, sliced
225g/8oz carrots, sliced
1 fennel bulb, sliced
675g/1½lb boneless hare, diced
30ml/2 tbsp plain (all-purpose) flour
60ml/4 tbsp Madeira
300ml/½ pint/1¼ cups game
   or chicken stock
45ml/3 tbsp chopped fresh parsley
450g/1lb puff pastry, thawed
   if frozen
beaten egg yolk, to glaze

VARIATION

You can make one large single pie, instead of four individual ones, if you like.

1 Heat 30ml/2 tbsp of the oil in a large pan. Add the leek, parsnips, carrots and fennel and cook for about 10 minutes, stirring frequently, until softened.

2 Using a slotted spoon, transfer the vegetables to the ceramic cooking pot. Cover with the lid and switch the slow cooker to the high or auto setting.

Nutritional information per portion: Energy 906Kcal/3784kJ; Protein 45g; Carbohydrate 60.4g, of which sugars 10g; Fat 53.7g, of which saturates 15.9g; Cholesterol 107mg; Calcium 180mg; Fibre 7.6g; Sodium 553mg.

MEAT DISHES

Slow cooking is suitable for all kinds of meat, but it works its magic best on less tender cuts, helping to improve and enhance their flavour and texture. Although beef and pork are great for robust dishes, such as steak and kidney pie, they can also be used to make lighter modern meals, like hot and sour pork. Most lamb cuts are naturally tender and succulent and the slow cooker ensures they stay that way – for a truly wonderful meal try lamb pie with mustard thatch. Whatever meat you choose and whether you are looking for a simple supper or an impressive dinner, you will find plenty of recipes here including a delicious pie, a braised dish, a casserole, hot-pots and stews.

STEAK and KIDNEY PIE with MUSTARD GRAVY

Peppery mustard gravy flavoured with bay leaves and parsley complements the tasty chunks of succulent beef and kidney in this classic pie. Cooking the puff pastry topping separately from the filling ensures it remains perfectly crisp – and is a perfect technique to use when making the pie using a slow cooker.

SERVES 4

675g/1½lb stewing steak
225g/8oz ox or lamb's kidney
45ml/3 tbsp oil
15g/½oz/1 tbsp unsalted (sweet) butter
2 onions, chopped
30ml/2 tbsp plain (all-purpose) flour
300ml/½ pint/1¼ cups beef stock
15ml/1 tbsp tomato purée (paste)
10ml/2 tsp English mustard
2 bay leaves
375g/13oz puff pastry
beaten egg, to glaze
15ml/1 tbsp chopped fresh parsley
salt and ground black pepper
creamed potatoes and green vegetables,
    to serve

1 Using a sharp knife, cut the stewing steak into 2.5cm/1in cubes. Remove all fat and skin from the kidney and cut into cubes or thick slices.

2 Heat 30ml/2 tbsp of the oil in a frying pan and brown the beef on all sides. Remove from the pan with a slotted spoon and place in the ceramic cooking pot. Switch the slow cooker on to high.

3 Add the kidney to the frying pan and brown for 1–2 minutes before adding to the beef. Add the remaining oil and the butter to the pan, add the onions and cook for 5 minutes, until just beginning to colour. Sprinkle with the flour and stir in, then remove the pan from the heat.

4 Gradually stir the stock into the pan, followed by the tomato purée and mustard. Return to the heat and bring to the boil, stirring constantly, until thickened. Pour the gravy over the meat, then add the bay leaves and season. Stir well and cover with the lid. Reduce the cooker to low and cook for 5–7 hours, or until the meat is very tender.

VARIATION

To make a richer version, use half the quantity of stock and add 150ml/¼ pint/ ⅔ cup stout or red wine.

5 While the beef is cooking, roll out the pastry and, using a dinner plate as a guide, cut out a 25cm/10in round. Transfer the pastry round to a baking sheet lined with baking parchment.

6 Using a sharp knife, mark the pastry into quarters, cutting almost but not quite through it. Decorate with pastry trimmings, then flute the edge. Cover with clear film (plastic wrap) and place in the refrigerator until ready to cook.

7 Towards the end of the beef's cooking time, preheat the oven to 200°C/400°F/ Gas 6. Brush the pastry all over with beaten egg to glaze, then bake for about 25 minutes, or until well risen, golden-brown and crisp.

8 To serve, stir the chopped parsley into the steak and kidney stew and spoon on to warmed serving plates. Cut the baked pie crust into four, using the markings as a guide, and top each portion of stew with a wedge of pastry. Serve immediately with rich, creamed potatoes and green vegetables.

Nutritional information per portion: Energy 637Kcal/2652kJ; Protein 18.7g; Carbohydrate 46.2g, of which sugars 5.2g; Fat 43.4g, of which saturates 13.1g; Cholesterol 259mg; Calcium 99mg; Fibre 2.7g; Sodium 578mg.

PROVENÇAL BEEF STEW

Known in France as daube de boeuf à la Provençal, *after the earthernware pot it was originally cooked in, this deliciously rich, fruity stew makes a perfect winter supper dish. Serve with mashed or boiled new potatoes and green vegetables.*

SERVES 4

45ml/3 tbsp olive oil
115g/4oz lean salt pork or
   thick-cut bacon, diced
900g/2lb stewing steak cut into
   4cm/1½in pieces
1 large onion, chopped
2 carrots, sliced
2 ripe tomatoes, peeled, seeded
   and chopped
10ml/2 tsp tomato purée (paste)
2 garlic cloves, very finely chopped
250ml/8fl oz/1 cup fruity red wine
150ml/¼ pint/⅔ cup beef stock
1 bouquet garni
1 small onion, studded with 2 cloves
grated zest and juice of ½ unwaxed orange
15ml/1 tbsp chopped fresh parsley
salt and ground black pepper

1 Heat 15ml/1 tbsp of the oil in a large heavy frying pan, then add the salt pork or bacon and cook over a medium heat for 4–5 minutes, stirring frequently, until browned and the fat is rendered.

2 Using a slotted spoon, transfer the pork or bacon to the ceramic cooking pot and switch the slow cooker to high.

3 Working in batches, add the beef to the pan in a single layer (do not overcrowd the pan, or the meat will stew in its own juices and not brown). Cook for 6–8 minutes until browned, turning to colour all sides.

4 Transfer the beef to the ceramic cooking pot and continue browning the rest of the meat in the same way, adding more oil when needed.

5 Pour the wine and stock over the beef in the ceramic cooking pot, then add the bouquet garni and the onion. Add the remaining oil and the onion to the frying pan and cook gently for 5 minutes. Stir in the carrots and cook for a further 5 minutes, until softened. Stir in the tomatoes, tomato purée and garlic, then transfer to the ceramic cooking pot.

6 Cover with the lid and switch the slow cooker to low. Cook for 5–7 hours, or until the beef and vegetables are very tender. Uncover and skim off any fat. Season, discard the bouquet garni and clove-studded onion, and stir in the orange zest and juice and the parsley.

Nutritional information per portion: Energy 547Kcal/2286kJ; Protein 55.8g; Carbohydrate 8.7g, of which sugars 7.2g; Fat 27.8g, of which saturates 8.9g; Cholesterol 170mg; Calcium 43mg; Fibre 2g; Sodium 682mg.

BRAISED BEEF in a RICH PEANUT SAUCE

Like many dishes brought to the Philippines by the Spanish, this slow-cooking Estofado,
renamed by the Philippinos as Kari Kari, retains much of its original charm. Peanuts are
used to thicken the juices, yielding a rich, sweet, glossy sauce.

SERVES 4

900g/2lb stewing (braising) chuck,
   shin or blade steak
45ml/3 tbsp vegetable oil
2 onions, chopped
2 cloves garlic, crushed
5ml/1 tsp paprika
pinch of ground turmeric
225g/8oz celeriac or swede (rutabaga),
   peeled and cut into 2cm/¾in dice
425ml/15fl oz/1¾ cups boiling beef stock
15ml/1 tbsp fish or anchovy sauce
30ml/2 tbsp tamarind sauce (optional)
10ml/2 tsp soft light brown sugar
1 bay leaf
1 sprig thyme
30ml/2 tbsp smooth peanut butter
45ml/3 tbsp easy-cook (converted)
   white rice
5ml/1 tsp white wine vinegar
salt and ground black pepper

1 Using a sharp knife, cut the beef into 2.5cm/1in cubes. Heat 30ml/2 tbsp of the oil in a pan and fry the beef, turning until well browned all over.

2 Transfer the meat and any juices to the ceramic cooking pot and switch the slow cooker to high.

3 Add the remaining 15ml/1 tbsp oil to the frying pan, add the onions and fry gently for 10 minutes until softened.

4 Add the garlic, paprika and turmeric to the pan and cook for 1 minute. Transfer the mixture to the ceramic pot and add the celeriac or swede.

5 Pour in the stock, fish or anchovy sauce and taramind sauce, if using, and add the sugar, bay leaf and thyme. Cover with the lid, then reduce the heat to low and cook for 4 hours, or until the beef and vegetables are just tender.

6 Turn the slow cooker up to high, then remove about 60ml/4 tbsp of the cooking juices to a bowl and blend with the peanut butter. Stir the mixture into the casserole, sprinkle with the rice, and stir again to combine.

7 Cover the pot and cook for about 45 minutes, or until the rice is cooked and the sauce has thickened slightly. Stir in the wine vinegar and season to taste.

COOK'S TIP
This stew makes a meal in itself so needs no accompaniments. However, a simple green salad served on the side makes a refreshing palate cleanser.

Nutritional information per portion: Energy 577Kcal/2408kJ; Protein 48.9g; Carbohydrate 14.1g, of which sugars 8.9g; Fat 36.8g, of which saturates 12.2g; Cholesterol 141mg; Calcium 70mg; Fibre 2.4g; Sodium 561mg.

HOT and SOUR PORK

This has all the flavour of a stir-fry without the hassle of last-minute cooking. Using lean pork fillet and reducing the temperature to low after an hour means that the meat remains wonderfully moist and tender, while the vegetables retain their crunchy texture.

SERVES 4

15ml/1 tbsp dried Chinese mushrooms
150ml/¼ pint/⅔ cup boiling
   vegetable stock
350g/12oz pork fillet
115g/4oz baby corn kernels
1 green (bell) pepper
225g/8oz pineapple chunks
   in natural juice
20ml/4 tsp cornflour (cornstarch)
15ml/1 tbsp sunflower oil
115g/4oz water chestnuts
2.5cm/1 in piece root ginger, grated
1 red chilli, seeded and finely chopped
5ml/1 tsp Chinese five-spice powder
15ml/1 tbsp sherry vinegar
15ml/1 tbsp dark soy sauce
15ml/1 tbsp hoisin sauce
plain boiled or fried rice, to serve

1 Put the mushrooms in a heatproof bowl, then pour over the hot stock and leave to soak for 15–20 minutes.

2 Trim away any visible fat from the pork and cut into 1cm/½ in slices. Slice the baby corn kernels lengthways. Halve, seed and slice the green pepper. Drain the pineapple chunks, reserving the juice. Drain the mushrooms, reserving the stock, and slice any large ones.

3 In a bowl, blend the cornflour with a little of the reserved pineapple juice, then slowly stir in the remainder.

4 Heat the oil in a non-stick frying pan. Add the pork and sear for 30 seconds on each side, or until lightly browned. Transfer to the ceramic cooking pot and add the vegetables, pineapple chunks and water chestnuts.

5 In a bowl, combine the ginger, chilli and five-spice powder with the vinegar, soy sauce, hoisin sauce and reserved stock. Pour in the pineapple juice mixture, then tip into the frying pan and bring to the boil, stirring constantly. As soon as the mixture thickens, pour over the pork and vegetables.

6 Cover with the lid and switch the slow cooker to high. Cook for 1 hour, then reduce the temperature to low and cook for 1–2 hours, or until the pork is cooked and the vegetables retain some crispness. Serve with rice.

Nutritional information per portion: Energy 358Kcal/1509kJ; Protein 19.9g; Carbohydrate 49.4g, of which sugars 36.3g; Fat 10.3g, of which saturates 2.8g; Cholesterol 60.4mg; Calcium 43mg; Fibre 2.7g; Sodium 405mg.

BOSTON BAKED BEANS

The slow cooker was actually invented for making baked beans. Molasses gives the beans a very rich flavour and dark colour, but you can replace it with maple syrup if you prefer.

SERVES 8

450g/1lb/2½ cups dried haricot
 (navy) beans
4 whole cloves
2 onions, peeled
1 bay leaf
90ml/6 tbsp tomato ketchup
30ml/2 tbsp molasses
30ml/2 tbsp dark brown sugar
15ml/1tbsp Dijon-style mustard
475ml/16fl oz/2 cups unsalted
 vegetable stock
225g/8oz piece of salt pork
salt and ground black pepper

1 Rinse the beans, then place in a large bowl. Cover with cold water and leave to soak for at least 8 hours or overnight.

2 Drain and rinse the beans. Place them in a large pan, cover with plenty of cold water and bring to the boil. Boil gently for about 10 minutes, then drain and tip into the ceramic cooking pot.

3 Stick 2 cloves in each of the onions. Add them to the pot with the bay leaf, burying them in the beans.

4 In a bowl, blend together the ketchup, molasses, sugar, mustard and stock, and pour over the beans. Add more stock, or water, if necessary, so that the beans are almost covered with liquid. Cover with the lid and switch the slow cooker to low. Cook for 3 hours.

5 Towards the end of the cooking time, place the salt pork in a pan of boiling water and cook for 3 minutes.

6 Using a sharp knife, score the pork rind in deep 1.5cm/½in cuts. Add the salt pork to the ceramic cooking pot, pushing it down just below the surface of the beans, skin side up. Cover the pot with the lid and cook for a further 5–6 hours, until the beans are tender.

7 Remove the pork from the beans and set aside until cool enough to handle, Using a sharp knife, slice off the rind and fat and finely slice the meat.

8 Using a spoon, skim off any fat from the top of the beans, then stir in the pieces of meat. Season to taste with salt and black pepper, and serve hot.

COOK'S TIPS
• Be sure to taste the beans before adding any more salt. The salt pork will have already added plenty, so you may only need to season with black pepper.
• To make a vegetarian version of these beans, simply leave out the salt pork. They are just as good cooked without.

Nutritional information per portion: Energy 228Kcal/968kJ; Protein 13.4g; Carbohydrate 43.9g, of which sugars 19.4g; Fat 1g, of which saturates 0.1g; Cholesterol 0mg; Calcium 140mg; Fibre 9.5g; Sodium 334mg.

POTATO and SAUSAGE CASSEROLE

There are many variations of this traditional Irish supper dish, known as Irish coddle, but the basic ingredients are the same wherever you go – potatoes, sausages and bacon.

SERVES 4

15ml/1 tbsp vegetable oil
8 large pork sausages
4 bacon rashers (slices), cut into 2.5cm/
 1in pieces
1 large onion, chopped
2 garlic cloves, crushed
4 large baking potatoes, peeled
 and thinly sliced
1.5ml/¼ tsp fresh sage
300ml/½ pint/1¼ cups vegetable stock
salt and ground black pepper

COOK'S TIPS

• For an authentic Irish feel, serve this delicious, hearty casserole with braised green cabbage.
• Choose good-quality sausages because it will make all the difference to the final result. Many Irish artisan butchers export quality Irish sausages, so it is well worth keeping an eye out for them.

1 Heat the oil in a frying pan. Gently fry the sausages for about 5 minutes, turning frequently until they are golden but not cooked through. Remove from the frying pan and set aside. Tip away all but about 10ml/2 tsp of fat from the pan.

2 Add the bacon to the pan and fry for 2 minutes. Add the onion and fry for about 8 minutes, stirring frequently until golden. Add the garlic and fry for a further 1 minute, then turn off the heat.

3 Arrange half the potato slices in the base of the ceramic cooking pot. Spoon the bacon and onion mixture on top. Season well with salt and ground black pepper, and sprinkle with the fresh sage. Cover with the remaining potato slices.

4 Pour the stock over the potatoes and top with the sausages. Cover with the lid and cook on high for 3–4 hours, or until the potatoes are tender and the sausages cooked through. Serve hot.

Nutritional information per portion: Energy 717Kcal/2984kJ; Protein 20.5g; Carbohydrate 49.9g, of which sugars 6.1g; Fat 49.8g, of which saturates 18.1g; Cholesterol 78.1mg; Calcium 73mg; Fibre 4g; Sodium 1322mg.

PORK and POTATO HOT-POT

Long, slow cooking makes the pork chops meltingly tender and allows the potato slices to soak up all the delicious juices from the meat. Perfect for a family meal or casual supper with friends, simply serve with lightly cooked green vegetables.

SERVES 4

25g/1oz/2 tbsp butter
15ml/1 tbsp oil
1 large onion, very thinly sliced
1 garlic clove, crushed
225g/8oz/generous 3 cups button (white)
  mushrooms, sliced
1.5ml/¼ tsp dried mixed herbs
900g/2lb potatoes, thinly sliced
4 thick pork chops
750ml/1¼ pints/3 cups vegetable
  or chicken stock
salt and ground black pepper

1 Use 15g/½oz/1 tbsp of the butter to grease the base and halfway up the sides of the ceramic cooking pot.

2 Heat the oil in a frying pan, add the sliced onion and cook gently for about 5 minutes, until softened and translucent.

3 Add the garlic and mushrooms to the pan and cook for a further 5 minutes until softened. Remove the pan from the heat and stir in the mixed herbs.

4 Spoon half the mushroom mixture into the base of the ceramic cooking pot, then arrange half the potato slices on top and season with salt and ground black pepper.

5 Using a sharp knife, trim as much fat as possible from the pork chops, then place them on top of the potatoes in a single layer. Pour about half the stock over the top to cover the potatoes and prevent them discolouring.

6 Repeat the layers of the mushroom mixture and potatoes, finishing with a layer of neatly overlapping potatoes. Pour over the remaining stock; it should just cover the potatoes, so use a little more or less if necessary. Dot the remaining butter on top of the potatoes and cover with the lid.

7 Cook the stew on high for 4–5 hours, or until the potatoes and meat are tender when pierced with a thin skewer. If you like, place the hot-pot under a medium grill (broiler) for 5–10 minutes to brown before serving.

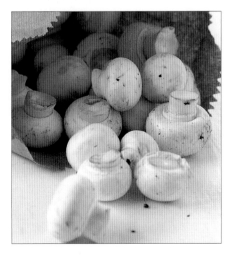

Nutritional information per portion: Energy 511Kcal/2132kJ; Protein 17.9g; Carbohydrate 41.5g, of which sugars 6.5g; Fat 31.5g, of which saturates 12.1g; Cholesterol 67mg; Calcium 40mg; Fibre 3.7g; Sodium 529mg.

CIDER-GLAZED GAMMON

This is a classic buffet centrepiece, which is ideal for Christmas or Thanksgiving. A fresh cranberry sauce provides the perfect foil to the richness of the meat and can be made in the slow cooker the day before if you want to serve the gammon hot, rather than cold. Soaking smoked gammon overnight helps to remove the excess salts.

SERVES 8

2kg/4½lb middle gammon joint, soaked
 overnight, if smoked
2 small onions
about 30 whole cloves
3 bay leaves
10 black peppercorns
150ml/¼ pint/⅔ cup medium-dry
 (medium-hard) cider
45ml/3 tbsp soft light brown sugar

For the cranberry sauce
350g/12oz/3 cups cranberries
175g/6oz/scant 1 cup caster (superfine)
 sugar
grated rind and juice of 2 clementines
30ml/2 tbsp port

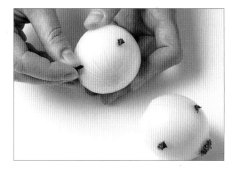

1 Drain the gammon joint, if soaked overnight, then place it in the ceramic cooking pot. Stud the onions with 6 of the cloves and add to the cooking pot with the bay leaves and peppercorns.

2 Pour over enough cold water to just cover the gammon. Switch the slow cooker to high, cover with the lid and cook for 1 hour. Skim off any scum from the surface, re-cover and cook for a further 4–5 hours. Check once during cooking and skim the surface, if necessary.

COOK'S TIP

The gammon should remain barely covered with water during cooking. There should be little evaporation from the slow cooker, but if necessary, top up with a small amount of boiling water.

3 Carefully lift the gammon joint out of the slow cooker using large forks or slotted spoons, and place it in a roasting tin (pan) or ovenproof dish. Leave to stand for about 15 minutes until cool enough to handle.

4 Meanwhile, make the glaze. Pour the cider into a small pan, add the soft brown sugar and heat gently, stirring, until dissolved. Simmer for 5 minutes to make a sticky glaze, then remove from the heat and leave to cool for a few minutes so that it thickens slightly.

5 Preheat the oven to 220°C/425°F/ Gas 7. Using a pair of scissors, snip the string off the gammon then carefully slice off the rind, leaving a thin, even layer of fat over the meat.

6 Using a sharp knife, score the fat into a neat diamond pattern. Press a clove into the centre of each diamond, then spoon over the glaze. Bake for about 25 minutes, or until the fat is brown, glistening and crisp. Remove from the oven and set aside until ready to serve.

7 Meanwhile, make the cranberry sauce. Wash the ceramic cooking pot, then add all the ingredients for the cranberry sauce to it. Switch the slow cooker to high and cook uncovered for 20 minutes, stirring continuously, until the sugar has dissolved completely.

8 Cover the pot with the lid and cook on high for 1½–2 hours, or until the cranberries are tender. Transfer the sauce to a jug (pitcher) or bowl, or keep warm in the slow cooker until ready to serve with the gammon. (The sauce can be served hot or cold.)

COOK'S TIPS

• If serving hot, cover the gammon with foil and leave to rest for 15 minutes before carving.
• If you prefer, serve the ham with redcurrant sauce or jelly. You can also use honey in place of the soft brown sugar for the glaze, if you like.

Nutritional information per portion: Energy 404Kcal/1689kJ; Protein 44.1g; Carbohydrate 15.2g, of which sugars 14.8g; Fat 18.8g, of which saturates 6.3g; Cholesterol 57mg; Calcium 25mg; Fibre 1g; Sodium 220mg.

VEAL STEW with TOMATOES

This classic French dish is traditionally made with lean and mildly flavoured veal.
Pork fillet makes an excellent, and economical, alternative.

SERVES 4

30ml/2 tbsp plain (all-purpose) flour
675g/1½lb boneless veal shoulder,
    trimmed and cut into cubes
30ml/2 tbsp sunflower oil
4 shallots, very finely chopped
300ml/½ pint/1¼ cups boiling vegetable
    or chicken stock
150ml/¼ pint/⅔ cup dry white wine
15ml/1 tbsp tomato purée (paste)
225g/8oz tomatoes, peeled, seeded
    and chopped
115g/4oz mushrooms, quartered
grated zest and juice of 1 small
    unwaxed orange
bouquet garni
salt and ground black pepper
30ml/2 tbsp chopped fresh parsley,
    to garnish

1 Put the flour in a small plastic bag and season with salt and pepper. Drop the pieces of meat into the bag a few at a time and shake to coat with the flour.

2 Heat 15ml/1 tbsp of the oil in a pan, add the shallots and cook gently for 5 minutes. Transfer to the ceramic cooking pot and switch to high or auto.

3 Add the remaining 15ml/1 tbsp oil to the pan and fry the meat in batches until well browned on all sides, then transfer to the ceramic cooking pot.

4 Pour the stock and white wine into the pan. Add the tomato purée and bring to the boil, stirring. Pour the sauce over the meat. Add the tomatoes, mushrooms, orange zest and juice, and bouquet garni to the pot and stir briefly to mix the ingredients. Cover with the lid and cook for about 1 hour.

5 Reduce the temperature to low or leave on auto and cook for 3–4 hours, or until the meat and mushrooms are very tender. Remove the bouquet garni, check the seasoning and add more salt and ground black pepper if necessary. Garnish with fresh parsley and serve.

Nutritional information per portion: Energy 323Kcal/1358kJ; Protein 38.2g; Carbohydrate 13.8g, of which sugars 5.4g; Fat 10.6g, of which saturates 2.3g; Cholesterol 141mg; Calcium 47mg; Fibre 1.7g; Sodium 314mg.

GREEK MEATBALLS in RICH TOMATO SAUCE

*There are many versions of these sausage-shaped meatballs, known as yiouvarlakia
or soudzoukakia. These are made with lamb, but beef makes an excellent alternative.*

SERVES 4

50g/2oz/1 cup fresh white breadcrumbs
1 egg, lightly beaten
finely grated rind of ½ small orange
2.5ml/½ tsp dried oregano
450g/1lb minced (ground) lamb
1 small onion, peeled and grated
2 cloves garlic, crushed
15ml/1 tbsp plain (all-purpose) flour
30ml/2 tbsp olive oil
salt and ground black pepper
flat leaf parsley, to garnish

For the sauce
1 onion, very finely chopped
400g/14oz can chopped tomatoes
150ml/¼ pint/⅔ cup hot lamb or beef
   stock
1 bay leaf

1 Put the breadcrumbs, beaten egg,
orange rind and oregano in a bowl and
stir together. Add the lamb, onion and
garlic and season with salt and pepper.
Mix together until thoroughly combined.

2 Using dampened hands, so that the
mixture doesn't stick, press the meat
mixture into small sausage-shapes, about
5cm/2in long, and roll them in flour.
Place in the refrigerator for 30 minutes
to firm up slightly.

COOK'S TIP
Serve these meatballs with a refreshing
salad and plenty of fresh, country-style
crusty bread for mopping up the juices.
Alternatively, serve with pitta bread so
that guests can stuff the breads with
meatballs and fresh green salad.

3 Heat the oil in a large frying pan and
add the meatballs, working in batches if
necessary. Cook for 5–8 minutes, turning
the meatballs, until evenly browned all
over. Transfer to a plate and set aside,
leaving the fat and juices in the pan.

4 To make the sauce, add the onion to
the pan and cook for 3–4 minutes, until
beginning to soften. Pour in the chopped
tomatoes, bring to the boil and cook
gently for 1 minute.

5 Transfer the sauce to the ceramic
cooking pot and stir in the stock. Add
the bay leaf and season with salt and
ground black pepper.

6 Arrange the meatballs in a single layer
in the sauce. Cover with the lid and
cook on high or auto for 1 hour. Reduce
the temperature to low or leave on auto
and cook for a further 4–5 hours. Serve
garnished with sprigs of fresh parsley.

Nutritional information per portion: Energy 363Kcal/1515kJ; Protein 26.1g; Carbohydrate 15g, of which sugars 5.3g; Fat 22.5g, of which saturates 8.3g; Cholesterol 141mg; Calcium 68mg; Fibre 1.5g; Sodium 239mg.

LANCASHIRE HOT-POT

This dish is traditionally made without browning the lamb or vegetables, and relies on long, slow cooking to develop the flavour. You can brown the top under the grill, if you like.

SERVES 4

8 middle neck or loin lamb chops,
    about 900g/2lb in total weight
900g/2lb potatoes, thinly sliced
2 onions, peeled and sliced
2 carrots, peeled and sliced
1 stick celery, trimmed and sliced
1 leek, peeled and sliced
225g/8oz/generous 3 cups button (white)
    mushrooms, sliced
5ml/1 tsp dried mixed herbs
small sprig of rosemary
475ml/16fl oz/2 cups lamb or beef stock
15g/½oz/1 tbsp butter, melted
salt and ground black pepper

3 Pour the meat stock into the ceramic cooking pot, then cover with the lid and switch the slow cooker to high or auto. Cook for 1 hour, then reduce the temperature to low or leave on auto and cook for 6–8 hours or until tender.

4 Brush the top layer of potatoes with melted butter. Place under a preheated grill (broiler) and cook for 5 minutes, or until the potatoes are lightly browned. Serve immediately.

1 Trim the lamb chops of excess fat. Place a layer of sliced potatoes in the base of the ceramic cooking pot, and top with some sliced vegetables and a sprinkling of dried herbs, salt and black pepper. Place four of the chops on top.

2 Repeat the layers of sliced potato, vegetables, dried herbs and meat, tucking the rosemary sprig down the side of the pot. Continue layering up the remaining vegetables, finishing with a neat layer of potatoes on the top.

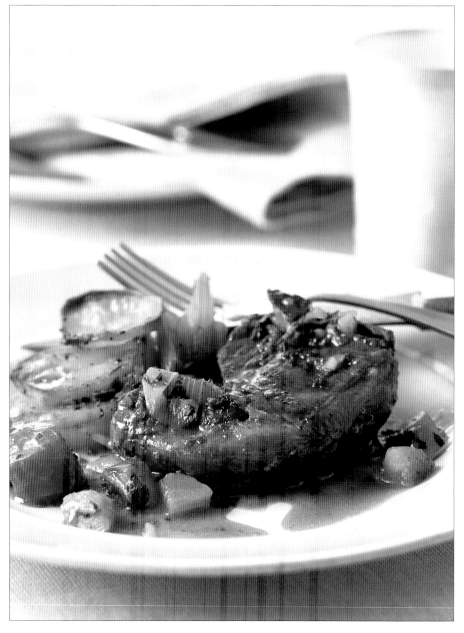

Nutritional information per portion: Energy 850Kcal/3544kJ; Protein 44.7g; Carbohydrate 45.3g, of which sugars 10.1g; Fat 55.8g, of which saturates 26.5g; Cholesterol 186mg; Calcium 72mg; Fibre 4.3g; Sodium 274mg.

LAMB PIE with MUSTARD THATCH

Here, a traditional shepherd's pie is given a contemporary twist with a tangy topping of mashed potato flavoured with peppery mustard. Serve with vegetables.

SERVES 4

450g/1lb lean minced (ground) lamb
1 onion, very finely chopped
2 celery sticks, thinly sliced
2 carrots, finely diced
15ml/1 tbsp cornflour (cornstarch)
    blended into 150ml/¼ pint/⅔ cup
    lamb stock
15ml/1 tbsp Worcestershire sauce
30ml/2 tbsp chopped fresh rosemary,
    or 10ml/2 tsp dried
800g/1¾lb floury potatoes, diced
60ml/4 tbsp milk
15ml/1 tbsp wholegrain mustard
25g/1oz/2 tbsp butter
salt and ground black pepper

1 Heat a non-stick frying pan, then add the lamb, breaking it up with a wooden spoon, and cook until lightly browned all over. Add the onion, celery and carrots to the pan and cook for 2–3 minutes, stirring frequently.

2 Stir the stock and cornflour mixture into the pan. Bring to the boil, stirring constantly, then remove from the heat. Stir in the Worcestershire sauce and rosemary, and season well with salt and ground black pepper.

3 Transfer the mixture to the ceramic cooking pot and switch the slow cooker to high. Cover and cook for 3 hours.

4 Towards the end of the cooking time, cook the potatoes in a large pan of boiling salted water until tender. Drain well, mash, and stir in the milk, mustard and butter. Season to taste.

5 Spoon the mashed potatoes on top of the lamb, spreading the mixture out evenly. Cook for a further 45 minutes. Brown the topping under a pre-heated grill (broiler) for a few minutes, if you like, then serve immediately.

Nutritional information per portion: Energy 458Kcal/1920kJ; Protein 26.5g; Carbohydrate 42.2g, of which sugars 8.1g; Fat 21.5g, of which saturates 10.6g; Cholesterol 101mg; Calcium 84mg; Fibre 3.5g; Sodium 264mg.

MOUSSAKA

This classic Greek dish topped with a light egg and cheese sauce is delicious in summer or winter, served with a crisp leafy salad. Try to find small, sweet aubergines with firm, shiny skins because they have much the best flavour. For an authentic touch, look out for Kefolotiri cheese in delicatessens and specialist food stores – although if you can't find it, Cheddar cheese will give equally good results.

SERVES 6

900g/2lb small or medium aubergines
   (eggplant), thinly sliced
60ml/4 tbsp olive oil
1 onion, finely chopped
2 garlic cloves, crushed
450g/1lb lean minced (ground) lamb
400g/14oz can chopped tomatoes
5ml/1 tsp dried oregano
pinch of ground cinnamon
salt and ground black pepper

For the topping
50g/2oz/¼ cup butter
50g/2oz/½ cup plain (all-purpose) flour
600ml/1 pint/2½ cups milk
pinch of freshly grated nutmeg
75g/3oz/¾ cup grated Kefolotiri or
   mature Cheddar cheese
1 egg yolk
30ml/2 tbsp fresh white breadcrumbs

1 Layer the aubergine slices in a sieve (strainer) or colander, sprinkling each layer with salt. Place the sieve over a bowl and leave to drain for 20 minutes. Rinse the aubergine slices thoroughly under cold running water and pat dry with kitchen paper.

VARIATION
You can use courgettes (zucchini) in place of the aubergines, if you prefer. Simply slice the courgettes, brush with olive oil and grill (broil) as before. There is no need to salt the courgette slices.

2 Lightly brush the aubergine slices with about half the oil, then arrange the slices in a single layer on a baking sheet. Place the baking sheet under a medium grill (broiler) and cook, turning once, until the aubergine slices are softened and golden brown on both sides.

3 Arrange half the aubergine slices in the bottom of the ceramic cooking pot and switch the slow cooker to high. Set aside the remaining slices.

4 Heat the remaining olive oil in a heavy pan, add the onion and fry gently for about 10 minutes, or until softened. Add the garlic and lamb and cook, stirring and breaking up the meat with a wooden spoon, until the meat is evenly browned.

5 Stir the tomatoes, oregano and cinnamon into the meat mixture, season generously with salt and ground black pepper and slowly bring to the boil over a gentle heat.

6 Spoon the lamb mixture into the slow cooker, covering the aubergine slices. Arrange the remaining aubergine slices on top, cover and cook for 2 hours.

7 Meanwhile, make the cheese topping. Melt the butter in a pan, stir in the flour and cook for one minute. Gradually stir in the milk, bring to the boil over a low heat, stirring constantly, and cook until thick and creamy. Lower the heat and simmer for 1 minute. Remove from the heat, season, then stir in the nutmeg and two-thirds of the cheese.

8 Leave the sauce to cool for 5 minutes, then beat in the egg yolk. Pour the sauce over the aubergine slices. Cover and cook for a further 2 hours, or until the topping is lightly set.

9 Sprinkle the remaining cheese and the breadcrumbs over the top and cook under a grill for 3–4 minutes, or until golden brown. Leave to stand for 5–10 minutes before serving.

Nutritional information per portion: Energy 444Kcal/1850kJ; Protein 24.1g; Carbohydrate 1.5g, of which sugars 11.2g; Fat 31g, of which saturates 14g; Cholesterol 93.5mg; Calcium 268mg; Fibre 4.1g; Sodium 266mg.

VEGETARIAN AND SIDE DISHES

Just because you follow a vegetarian diet, it doesn't mean you will miss out on fabulous-tasting food. This chapter makes use of all kinds of wonderful vegetables, beans and grains to make fabulous slow-cooked main meals that will appeal just as much to meat-eaters as they do to vegetarians. Try rich and creamy coconut, tomato and lentil dhal or sweet and sour mixed-bean hot-pot for a hearty main meal. Or if you are looking for something a little less substantial, try baked eggs with creamy leeks. Whatever you are in the mood for, you are sure to find the perfect meat-free recipe in this chapter.

BAKED EGGS with CREAMY LEEKS

Enjoy these deliciously creamy eggs for a light lunch or supper with toast and a salad.
You can use other vegetables in place of the leeks, such as puréed spinach or ratatouille.

3 Melt the butter in a small frying pan and cook the leeks over a medium heat, stirring frequently, until softened.

4 Add 45ml/3 tbsp of the cream and cook gently for about 5 minutes, or until the leeks are very soft and the cream has thickened a little. Season with salt, black pepper and nutmeg.

5 Spoon the leeks into the ramekins or soufflé dishes, dividing the mixture equally. Using the back of the spoon, make a hollow in the centre of each pile of leeks, then break an egg into the hollow. Spoon 5–10ml/1–2 tsp of the remaining cream over each egg and season lightly with salt and pepper.

6 Cover each dish with clear film (plastic wrap) and place in the slow cooker. If necessary, pour in a little more boiling water to come halfway up the sides of the dishes. Cover and cook for 30 minutes, or until the egg whites are set and the yolks are still soft, or a little longer if you prefer the eggs firmer.

SERVES 4

15g/½oz/1 tbsp butter, plus extra
  for greasing
225g/8oz small leeks, thinly sliced
60–90ml/4–6 tbsp whipping or double
  (heavy) cream
freshly grated nutmeg
4 eggs
salt and ground black pepper

VARIATION
To make herb and cheese eggs, put 15ml/
1 tbsp double (heavy) cream in each dish
with some chopped herbs. Break in the
eggs, add 15ml/1 tbsp double cream and
a little grated cheese, then cook as
before. This is the perfect recipe for
a lazy weekend brunch.

1 Pour about 2.5cm/1in hot water into the ceramic cooking pot and switch the slow cooker to high.

2 Using a pastry brush, lightly butter the base and insides of four 175ml/ 6fl oz/¾ cup ramekins or individual soufflé dishes.

SAVOURY NUT LOAF

Ideal as an alternative to the traditional meat roast, this wholesome dish is perfect for special occasions. It is also particularly good served with a spicy fresh tomato sauce.

SERVES 4

30ml/2 tbsp olive oil, plus extra
    for greasing
1 onion, finely chopped
1 leek, finely chopped
2 celery sticks, finely chopped
225g/8oz/3 cups mushrooms, chopped
2 garlic cloves, crushed
425g/15oz can lentils, rinsed and drained
115g/4oz/1 cup mixed nuts, such as
    hazelnuts, cashew nuts and almonds,
    finely chopped
50g/2oz/½ cup plain (all-purpose) flour
50g/2oz/½ cup grated mature (sharp)
    Cheddar cheese
1 egg, beaten
45–60ml/3–4 tbsp chopped fresh
    mixed herbs
salt and ground black pepper
chives and sprigs of fresh flat leaf parsley,
    to garnish

1 Place an upturned saucer or metal pastry ring in the base of the ceramic cooking pot. Pour in about 2.5cm/1in hot water and switch the slow cooker to high.

2 Lightly grease the base and sides of a 900g/2lb loaf tin (pan) or terrine – first making sure it will fit in the slow cooker – and line the base and sides of the tin with baking parchment.

3 Heat the oil in a large pan, add the onion, leek, celery, mushrooms and garlic, then cook for 10 minutes, until the vegetables have softened. Do not let them brown.

4 Remove the pan from the heat, then stir in the lentils, mixed nuts and flour, grated cheese, beaten egg and herbs. Season well with salt and black pepper and mix thoroughly.

5 Spoon the nut mixture into the prepared loaf tin or terrine, pressing right into the corners. Level the surface with a fork, then cover the tin with a piece of foil. Place the loaf tin in the ceramic cooking pot and pour in enough near-boiling water to come just over halfway up the side of the dish.

6 Cover the slow cooker with the lid and cook for 3–4 hours, or until the loaf is firm to the touch.

7 Leave the loaf to cool in the tin for about 15 minutes, then turn out on to a serving plate. Serve the loaf hot or cold, cut into thick slices and garnished with fresh chives and sprigs of flat leaf parsley.

Nutritional information per portion: Energy 484Kcal/2019kJ; Protein 23.7g; Carbohydrate 34.1g, of which sugars 5.1g; Fat 29g, of which saturates 5.4g; Cholesterol 69mg; Calcium 238mg; Fibre 8.7g; Sodium 128mg.

MUSHROOM and FENNEL HOT-POT

Hearty and richly flavoured, this tasty stew makes a marvellous vegetarian main dish, but it can also be served as an accompaniment to meat dishes. Dried mushrooms swell up a great deal after soaking, so a little goes a long way in terms of both flavour and quantity.

SERVES 4

25g/1oz/½ cup dried shiitake mushrooms
1 small head of fennel
30ml/2 tbsp olive oil
12 shallots, peeled
225g/8oz/3 cups button (white)
   mushrooms, trimmed and halved
250ml/8fl oz/1 cup dry (hard) cider
25g/1oz/½ cup sun-dried tomatoes
30ml/2 tbsp/½ cup sun-dried
   tomato paste
1 bay leaf
salt and ground black pepper
chopped fresh parsley,
   to garnish

1 Place the dried shiitake mushrooms in a heatproof bowl. Pour over just enough hot water to cover them and leave to soak for about 15 minutes. Meanwhile, trim and slice the fennel.

2 Heat the oil in a heavy pan. Add the shallots and fennel, then sauté for about 10 minutes over a medium heat, until the vegetables are softened and just beginning to brown. Add the button mushrooms to the pan and cook for a further 2–3 minutes, stirring occasionally.

3 Transfer the vegetable mixture to the ceramic cooking pot. Drain the shiitake mushrooms, adding 30ml/2 tbsp of the soaking liquid to the cooking pot. Chop them and add them to the pot.

4 Pour the cider into the pot and stir in the sun-dried tomatoes and tomato paste. Add the bay leaf. Cover with the lid and cook on high for 3–4 hours, or until the vegetables are tender.

5 Remove the bay leaf and season to taste with salt and black pepper. Serve sprinkled with plenty of chopped parsley.

Nutritional information per portion: Energy 94Kcal/394kJ; Protein 2.1g; Carbohydrate 4.2g, of which sugars 4g; Fat 6g, of which saturates 0.9g; Cholesterol 0mg; Calcium 28mg; Fibre 2.4g; Sodium 17mg.

SWEET and SOUR MIXED-BEAN HOT-POT

This impressive-looking dish, topped with sliced potatoes, is incredibly easy, making the most of dried and canned ingredients from the kitchen cupboard and combining them with a deliciously rich and tangy tomato sauce.

SERVES 6

40g/1½oz/3 tbsp butter
4 shallots, peeled and finely chopped
40g/1½oz/⅓ cup plain (all-purpose)
    or wholemeal (whole-wheat) flour
300ml/½ pint/1¼ cups passata (bottled
    strained tomatoes)
120ml/4fl oz/½ cup unsweetened
    apple juice
60ml/4 tbsp soft light brown sugar
60ml/4 tbsp tomato ketchup
60ml/4 tbsp dry sherry
60ml/4 tbsp cider vinegar
60ml/4 tbsp light soy sauce
400g/14oz can butter beans
400g/14oz can flageolet (small cannellini)
    beans
400g/14oz can chickpeas
175g/6oz green beans, cut into 2.5cm/
    1in lengths
225g/8oz/3 cups mushrooms, sliced
450g/1lb unpeeled potatoes
15ml/1 tbsp olive oil
15ml/1 tbsp chopped fresh thyme
15ml/1 tbsp fresh marjoram
salt and ground black pepper
fresh herbs, to garnish

1 Melt the butter in a pan, add the shallots and fry gently for 5–6 minutes, until softened. Add the flour and cook for 1 minute, stirring all the time, then gradually stir in the passata.

2 Add the apple juice, sugar, tomato ketchup, sherry, vinegar and light soy sauce to the pan and stir in. Bring the mixture to the boil, stirring constantly until it thickens.

VARIATIONS
• You can vary the proportions and types of beans used, depending on what you have in the store cupboard (pantry). Kidney beans and borlotti beans would work well and can be either interchanged with any of the beans used here, or combined with them.
• Try using mangetout (snow peas) in place of the green beans, if you prefer.

3 Rinse the beans and chickpeas and drain well. Place them in the ceramic cooking pot with the green beans and mushrooms and pour over the sauce. Stir well, then cover with the lid and cook on high for 3 hours.

4 Meanwhile, thinly slice the potatoes and par-boil them for 4 minutes. Drain well, then toss them in the oil so that they are lightly coated all over.

5 Stir the fresh herbs into the bean mixture and season with salt and pepper. Arrange the potato slices on top of the beans, overlapping them slightly so that they completely cover them. Cover the pot and cook for a further 2 hours, or until the potatoes are tender.

6 Place the ceramic cooking pot under a medium grill (broiler) and cook for 4–5 minutes to brown the potato topping. Serve garnished with herbs.

Nutritional information per portion: Energy 483Kcal/2042kJ; Protein 18.5g; Carbohydrate 73.3g, of which sugars 24.8g; Fat 13.8g, of which saturates 4.5g; Cholesterol 14mg; Calcium 134mg; Fibre 10.9g; Sodium 826mg.

MUSHROOM AND COURGETTE LASAGNE

This is the perfect main-course lasagne for vegetarians. Adding dried porcini to fresh chestnut mushrooms intensifies the flavour. The dish can be made and assembled in the slow cooker early in the day, then left to cook. Serve with crusty Italian bread.

SERVES 6

For the tomato sauce
15g/½oz dried porcini mushrooms
120ml/4fl oz/½ cup hot water
1 onion
1 carrot
1 celery stick
30ml/2 tbsp olive oil
2 x 400g/14oz cans chopped tomatoes
15ml/1 tbsp sun-dried tomato paste
5ml/1 tsp granulated sugar
5ml/1 tsp dried basil or mixed herbs

For the lasagne
30ml/2 tbsp olive oil
50g/2oz/¼ cup butter
450g/1lb courgettes (zucchini), thinly sliced
1 onion, finely chopped
450g/1lb/6 cups chestnut mushrooms, thinly sliced
2 garlic cloves, crushed
6–8 non-pre-cook lasagne sheets
50g/2oz/½ cup freshly grated Parmesan cheese
salt and ground black pepper
fresh oregano leaves, to garnish
Italian-style bread, to serve (optional)

For the white sauce
40g/1½oz/3 tbsp butter
40g/1½oz/⅓ cup plain (all-purpose) flour
900ml/1½ pints/3¾ cups milk
freshly grated nutmeg

1 Put the dried porcini mushrooms in a bowl. Pour over the hot water and leave to soak for 15 minutes. Tip the porcini and liquid into a sieve (strainer) set over a bowl and squeeze the mushrooms with your hands to release as much liquid as possible. Chop the mushrooms finely and set aside. Strain the soaking liquid through a fine sieve and reserve.

2 Chop the onion, carrot and celery finely. Heat the olive oil in a pan and fry the vegetables until softened. Place in a food processor with the tomatoes, tomato paste, sugar, herbs, porcini and soaking liquid, and blend to a purée.

3 For the lasagne, heat the olive oil and half the butter in a large pan. Add half the courgette slices and season to taste. Cook over a medium heat, turning the courgettes frequently, for 5–8 minutes, until lightly coloured on both sides. Remove from the pan with a slotted spoon and transfer to a bowl. Repeat with the remaining courgettes.

4 Melt the remaining butter in the pan, and cook the onion for 3 minutes, stirring. Add the chestnut mushrooms, chopped porcini and garlic and cook for 5 minutes. Add to the courgettes.

5 For the white sauce, melt the butter in a large pan, then add the flour and cook, stirring, for 1 minute. Turn off the heat and gradually whisk in the milk. Bring to the boil and cook, stirring, until the sauce is smooth and thick. Season with salt, black pepper and nutmeg.

6 Ladle half of the tomato sauce into the ceramic cooking pot and spread out to cover the base. Add half the vegetable mixture, spreading it evenly. Top with about one-third of the white sauce, then about half the lasagne sheets, breaking them to fit the cooking pot. Repeat these layers, then top with the remaining white sauce and sprinkle with grated Parmesan cheese.

7 Cover the ceramic cooking pot with the lid and cook on low for 2–2½ hours or until the lasagne is tender. If you like, brown the top under a medium grill (broiler). Garnish with a sprinkling of fresh oregano leaves, and serve with fresh Italian-style bread.

Nutritional information per portion: Energy 421Kcal/1757kJ; Protein 15.5g; Carbohydrate 32.9g, of which sugars 15g; Fat 26.2g, of which saturates 12.4g; Cholesterol 49mg; Calcium 346mg; Fibre 3.8g; Sodium 310mg.

COUSCOUS-STUFFED SWEET PEPPERS

The peppers are softened in boiling water before filling to ensure really tender results.
Choose red, yellow or orange peppers for this dish, but avoid green ones because they
tend to discolour after a couple of hours of cooking and do not have such a sweet taste.

SERVES 4

4 (bell) peppers
75g/3oz/½ cup instant couscous
75ml/2½fl oz/⅓ cup boiling
    vegetable stock
15ml/1 tbsp olive oil
10ml/2 tsp white wine vinegar
50g/2oz dried apricots, finely chopped
75g/3oz feta cheese, cut into tiny cubes
3 ripe tomatoes, skinned, seeded
    and chopped
45ml/3 tbsp toasted pine nuts
30ml/2 tbsp chopped fresh parsley
salt and ground black pepper
flat leaf parsley, to garnish

1 Halve the peppers lengthways, then
remove the core and seeds. Place the
peppers in a large heatproof bowl and
pour over boiling water to cover. Leave
to stand for about 3 minutes, then drain
thoroughly and set aside.

2 Meanwhile, put the couscous in a
small bowl and pour over the stock.
Leave to stand for about 5 minutes until
all the water has been absorbed.

3 Using a fork, fluff up the couscous,
then stir in the oil, vinegar, apricots, feta
cheese, tomatoes, pine nuts and parsley,
and season to taste with salt and ground
black pepper.

COOK'S TIP
Be sure to taste the stuffing before adding
any more salt. Feta cheese can be very
salty already, so you may not need to
add any extra.

4 Fill the peppers with the couscous
mixture, gently packing it down using
the back of a spoon.

5 Place the peppers, filling side up,
in the ceramic cooking pot, then
pour 150ml/¼ pint/⅔ cup near-boiling
water around them.

6 Cover with the lid, switch the slow
cooker to high and cook for 2–3 hours,
or until the peppers are tender. Brown
under a hot grill (broiler) for 2 minutes
and serve garnished with fresh parsley.

Nutritional information per portion: Energy 303Kcal/1266kJ; Protein 33.7g; Carbohydrate 33.6g, of which sugars 17g; Fat 15.8g, of which saturates 3.9g; Cholesterol 13mg; Calcium 105mg; Fibre 4.3g; Sodium 285mg.

COCONUT, TOMATO and LENTIL DHAL with TOASTED ALMONDS

Richly flavoured and utterly moreish, this lentil dish makes a filling supper served with warm naan bread and plain yogurt. Split red lentils give the dish a vibrant colour, but you could use larger yellow split peas instead, although they will take a little longer to cook.

SERVES 4

30ml/2 tbsp vegetable oil
1 large onion, very finely chopped
3 garlic cloves, chopped
1 carrot, diced
10ml/2 tsp cumin seeds
10ml/2 tsp yellow mustard seeds
2.5cm/1in piece fresh root ginger, grated
10ml/2 tsp ground turmeric
5ml/1 tsp mild chilli powder
5ml/1 tsp garam masala
225g/8oz/1 cup split red lentils
400ml/14fl oz/1⅔ cup boiling
    vegetable stock
400ml/14fl oz/1⅔ cups coconut milk
5 tomatoes, peeled, seeded and chopped
juice of 2 limes
60ml/4 tbsp chopped fresh coriander
    (cilantro)
salt and ground black pepper
25g/1oz/¼ cup flaked (sliced) almonds,
    toasted, to garnish

1 Heat the oil in a pan. Add the onion and cook for 5 minutes, until softened, stirring occasionally.

2 Add the garlic, carrot, cumin, mustard seeds and ginger to the pan. Cook for 3–4 minutes, stirring, until the seeds begin to pop, the aromas are released and the carrot softens slightly.

COOK'S TIP
This dish reheats well, so it is worth making a double batch and freezing half. Thaw, then add a little water and reheat.

3 Add the ground turmeric, chilli powder and garam masala to the pan and cook, stirring, for 1 minute, or until the flavours begin to mingle.

4 Tip the mixture into the ceramic cooking pot. Add the lentils, stock, coconut milk and tomatoes and season with salt and pepper. Stir well and cover the pot with the lid.

5 Cook on high for 2 hours, or until the lentils are soft, stirring halfway through the cooking time to prevent the lentils sticking. Stir the lime juice and 45ml/3 tbsp of fresh coriander into the dhal.

6 Check the seasoning and cook for a further 30 minutes. To serve, sprinkle with the remaining fresh coriander and the toasted almonds.

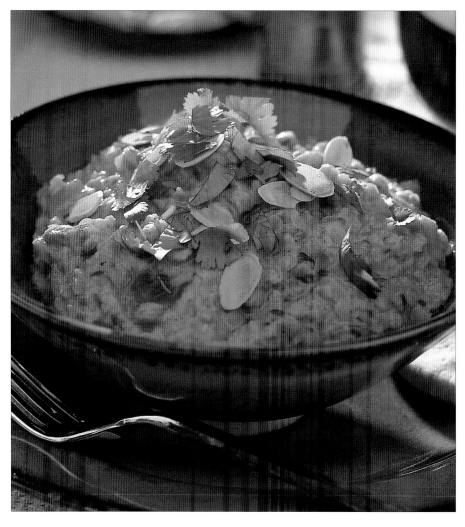

Nutritional information per portion: Energy 335Kcal/1421kJ; Protein 16.6g; Carbohydrate 46.3g, of which sugars 14.3g; Fat 10.6g, of which saturates 1.4g; Cholesterol 0mg; Calcium 99mg; Fibre 5.5g; Sodium 230mg.

POTATO, ONION and GARLIC GRATIN

This tasty side dish makes the perfect accompaniment to roasts, stews and grilled meat or fish. Cooking the potatoes in stock with onions and garlic gives them a really rich flavour.

3 Pour just enough of the stock into the pot to cover the potatoes. Cover with the lid and cook on low for 8–10 hours, or on high for 4–5 hours, until the potatoes are tender.

4 If you like, brown the potatoes under a hot grill (broiler) for 3–4 minutes. Serve sprinkled with a little salt and ground black pepper.

VARIATIONS

• To make this dish more substantial, sprinkle 115g/4oz/1 cup of grated Gruyère cheese over the top of the cooked potatoes and brown under a preheated grill (broiler) for 3–4 minutes until golden-brown and bubbling.
• Alternatively, crumble 165g/5½oz/scant 1 cup soft goat's cheese on the gratin 30 minutes before the end of cooking.
• To vary the flavour, try using chopped rosemary or sage in place of the thyme, or use crushed juniper berries instead.

SERVES 4

40g/1½oz/3 tbsp butter
1 large onion, finely sliced into rings
2–4 garlic cloves, finely chopped
2.5ml/½ tsp dried thyme
900g/2lb waxy potatoes, very finely sliced
450ml/¾ pint/scant 2 cups boiling
vegetable, chicken, beef or
lamb stock
sea salt and ground black pepper

1 Grease the inside of the ceramic cooking pot with 15g/½oz/1 tbsp of the butter. Spoon a thin layer of onions on to the base of the cooking pot, then sprinkle over a little of the chopped garlic, thyme, salt and pepper.

2 Carefully arrange an overlapping layer of potato slices on top of the onion mixture in the ceramic cooking pot. Continue to layer the ingredients in the pot until all the onions, garlic, herbs and potatoes are used up, finishing with a layer of sliced potatoes.

Nutritional information per portion: Energy 260Kcal/1092kJ; Protein 5.1g; Carbohydrate 41.9g, of which sugars 6.4g; Fat 9.1g, of which saturates 5.4g; Cholesterol 21mg; Calcium 31mg; Fibre 3.3g; Sodium 171mg.

DESSERTS AND CAKES

From baked custard and poached fruit to steamed puddings and luscious cakes, this tempting chapter is perfect for anyone with a sweet tooth. Try old-fashioned favourites such as poached pears in red wine, baked stuffed apples, and hot bananas with rum and raisins, or indulge yourself with a really wicked treat such as sticky coffee and pear pudding or Vermont baked maple custard. When you are looking for a little something to enjoy in the afternoon with a cup of tea or coffee, try any one of the fabulous cakes – frosted carrot and parsnip cake, chocolate chip walnut cake or moist golden ginger cake. One mouthful of any of these and you will be in heaven.

BAKED STUFFED APPLES

Using Italian amaretti to stuff the apples gives a lovely almondy flavour, while dried cranberries and glacé fruit add sweetness and colour. Make sure that you choose a variety of apple that will remain firm during the long cooking time.

3 Add the nuts and dried cranberries or sour cherries and glacé fruit to the bowl and mix well, then set aside the filling while you prepare the apples.

4 Wash and dry the apples. Remove the cores using an apple corer, then carefully enlarge each core cavity to twice its size, using the corer to shave out more flesh. Using a sharp knife, score each apple around its equator.

5 Divide the filling among the apples, packing it into the hole, then piling it on top. Stand the apples in the cooking pot and cover with the lid. Reduce the temperature to low and cook for 4 hours, or until tender. Transfer the apples to warmed serving plates and spoon the sauce over the top. Serve with cream, crème fraîche or vanilla ice cream.

SERVES 4

75g/3oz/6 tbsp butter, softened
45ml/3 tbsp orange or apple juice
75g/3oz/scant ½ cup light muscovado (brown) sugar
grated rind and juice of ½ orange
1.5ml/¼ tsp ground cinnamon
30ml/2 tbsp crushed amaretti
25g/1oz/¼ cup pecan nuts, chopped
25g/1oz/¼ cup dried cranberries or sour cherries
25g/1oz/¼ cup luxury mixed glacé (candied) fruit, chopped
4 large cooking apples, such as Bramleys
cream, crème fraîche or vanilla ice cream, to serve

1 Grease the ceramic cooking pot with 15g/½oz/1 tbsp of the butter, then pour in the fruit juice and switch to high.

2 Put the remaining butter, the sugar, orange rind and juice, cinnamon and amaretti crumbs in a bowl and mix well.

COOK'S TIP
The cooking time will depend on the type and size of apples used.

Nutritional information per portion: Energy 347Kcal/1457kJ; Protein 1.6g; Carbohydrate 42.4g, of which sugars 41.3g; Fat 20.3g, of which saturates 10.3g; Cholesterol 40mg; Calcium 27mg; Fibre 3g; Sodium 131mg.

POACHED PEARS in RED WINE

The pears take on a red blush from the wine and make a very pretty dessert. It works best in a small slow cooker, which ensures that the pears stay submerged during cooking.

SERVES 4

1 bottle fruity red wine
150g/5oz/¾ cup caster (superfine) sugar
45ml/3 tbsp clear honey
1 cinnamon stick
1 vanilla pod (bean), split lengthwise
large strip of lemon or orange rind
2 whole cloves
2 black peppercorns
4 firm ripe pears
juice of ½ lemon
mint leaves, to garnish
whipped cream or sour cream, to serve

1 Pour the red wine into the ceramic cooking pot. Add the sugar, honey, cinnamon stick, vanilla pod, lemon or orange rind, cloves and peppercorns. Cover with the lid and cook on high for 30 minutes, stirring occasionally.

2 Meanwhile, peel the pears using a vegetable peeler, leaving the stem intact. Take a very thin slice off the base of each pear so it will stand square and upright. As each pear is peeled, toss it in the lemon juice to prevent the flesh browning when exposed to the air.

3 Place the pears in the spiced wine mixture. Cover with the lid and cook for 2–4 hours, turning the pears occasionally, until they are just tender; be careful not to overcook them.

COOK'S TIP
The cooking time will depend on the size and ripeness of the pears. Small, ripe pears will cook quickly; large, hard pears will take longer.

4 Transfer the pears to a bowl using a slotted spoon. Continue to cook the wine mixture uncovered for a further hour, until reduced and thickened a little, then turn off the slow cooker and leave to cool. Alternatively, to save time, pour the cooking liquor into a pan and boil briskly for 10–15 minutes.

5 Strain the cooled liquid over the pears and chill for at least 3 hours. Place the pears in four individual serving dishes and spoon a little of the wine syrup over each one. Garnish with fresh mint and serve with whipped or sour cream.

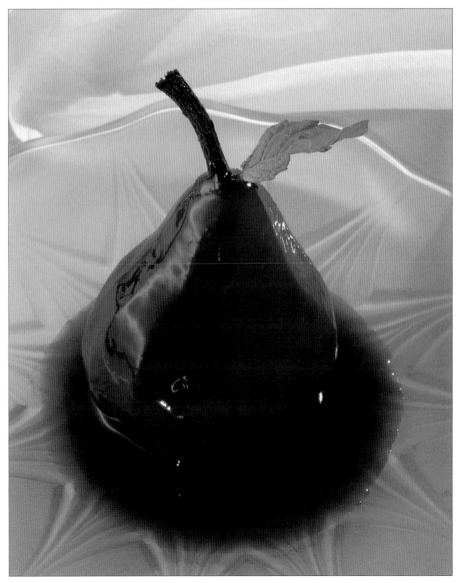

Nutritional information per portion: Energy 87Kcal/367kJ; Protein 0.5g; Carbohydrate 16.6g, of which sugars 16.6g; Fat 0.2g, of which saturates 0g; Cholesterol 0mg; Calcium 19mg; Fibre 3.3g; Sodium 7mg.

VERMONT BAKED MAPLE CUSTARD

Maple syrup has a really distinctive flavour and gives these little baked custards a wonderfully rich taste. Try to find pure maple syrup – it will make all the difference.

SERVES 6

3 eggs
120ml/4fl oz/½ cup maple syrup
250ml/8fl oz/1 cup warm milk
150ml/¼ pint/⅔ cup warm single
    (light) cream
5ml/1 tsp vanilla extract
whole nutmeg, to grate

COOK'S TIP
Warming the milk and cream until tepid will help the custard cook and set more quickly. You can do this in a pan on the stovetop, or more simply, pour the milk and cream into a heatproof bowl or jug (pitcher) and place in the slow cooker filled with near-boiling water to a depth of about 5cm/2in. Switch the slow cooker to high and leave for 30 minutes. Remove the milk, then turn the slow cooker to low and use the hot water in the ceramic cooking pot to cook the custards.

1 Beat the eggs in a large bowl, then whisk in the maple syrup, followed by the warm milk, cream and the vanilla extract. Grate in a little nutmeg.

2 Strain the custard mixture into six individual ramekins – first checking that the dishes will all fit inside the ceramic cooking pot in a single layer. Carefully cover each ramekin with a piece of kitchen foil, then place them in the ceramic cooking pot.

3 Pour very hot water around the dishes to come three-quarters of the way up their sides. Cover with the lid and cook on low for 2½–3 hours, or until set. To test, insert a skewer in the middle; it should come out clean.

4 Transfer the custards to a wire rack. Leave for 5 minutes and serve warm, or leave to cool completely, then chill. Remove from the refrigerator about 30 minutes before serving.

Nutritional information per portion: Energy 174Kcal/735kJ; Protein 8.6g; Carbohydrate 24.5g, of which sugars 18.7g; Fat 5.3g, of which saturates 1.6g; Cholesterol 116mg; Calcium 97mg; Fibre 9.1g; Sodium 120mg.

HOT BANANAS with RUM and RAISINS

*These sticky, sweet baked bananas are utterly moreish and make a great dessert all
year round. The rich sauce becomes almost toffee-like during cooking, and is irresistible.*

3 Add the bananas to the melted butter
and sugar mixture, cover with the lid and
cook for about 30 minutes, or until the
fruit is almost tender, turning over the
bananas halfway through cooking time.

4 Sprinkle the nutmeg and cinnamon
over the bananas, then pour in the rum
and raisins. Stir very gently to mix, then
re-cover and cook for 10 minutes.

5 Carefully lift the bananas out of the
ceramic cooking pot and arrange on
a serving dish or individual plates.
Spoon over the sauce, then sprinkle
with almonds, if using. Serve hot with
whipped cream or vanilla ice cream.

COOK'S TIP

Choose almost-ripe bananas with even-
coloured skins. Over-ripe bananas will
not hold their shape during cooking, and
will give mushy results.

SERVES 4

30ml/2 tbsp seedless raisins
45ml/3 tbsp dark rum
40g/1½oz/3 tbsp unsalted (sweet) butter
50g/2oz/¼ cup soft light brown sugar
4 slightly under-ripe bananas, peeled and
    halved lengthways
1.5ml/¼ tsp grated nutmeg
1.5ml/¼ tsp ground cinnamon
25g/1oz/¼ cup flaked (sliced) almonds,
    toasted (optional)
whipped cream or vanilla ice cream,
    to serve

1 Put the raisins in a bowl and spoon
over 30ml/2 tbsp of the rum. Set aside
and leave to soak.

2 Cut the butter into small cubes and
place in the ceramic cooking pot with
the sugar and remaining 15ml/1 tbsp
rum. Switch the slow cooker to high
and leave uncovered for 15 minutes,
until the butter and sugar have melted.

VARIATION

If you don't like the taste of rum, try
using an orange liqueur, such as Cointreau,
instead. It makes a very good alternative
and is a little less overpowering.

Nutritional information per portion: Energy 323Kcal/1355kJ; Protein 3g; Carbohydrate 47.1g, of which sugars 44.7g; Fat 12.1g, of which saturates 5.6g; Cholesterol 21mg; Calcium 33mg; Fibre 1.9g; Sodium 72mg.

STICKY COFFEE and PEAR PUDDING

This dark and moist fruity pudding is complemented with a tangy citrus-flavoured cream.
It is delicious served hot, but is equally good cold; serve at room temperature rather than
chilled to enjoy its rich flavour and wonderful texture at their best.

SERVES 6

115g/4oz/½ cup butter, softened, plus
    extra for greasing
30ml/2 tbsp ground coffee
15ml/1 tbsp near-boiling water
50g/2oz/½ cup toasted skinned hazelnuts
4 small ripe pears
juice of ½ orange
115g/4oz/generous ½ cup golden caster
    (superfine) sugar, plus 15ml/1 tbsp for
    baking
2 eggs, beaten
50g/2oz/½ cup self-raising (self-rising) flour
45ml/3 tbsp maple syrup
fine strips of orange rind, to decorate

For the orange cream
300ml/½ pint/1¼ cups whipping cream
15ml/1 tbsp icing (confectioners') sugar,
    sifted
finely grated rind of ½ orange

1 Pour about 2.5cm/1in of hot water
into the ceramic cooking pot. Place an
upturned saucer or metal pastry ring in
the base, then turn on to high. Grease
and line the base of a deep 18cm/7in
fixed-base cake tin (pan) or soufflé dish.

COOK'S TIPS
• If you can't find ready-toasted skinned
hazelnuts, prepare your own. Toast the
nuts under a hot grill (broiler) for about
3 minutes, turning frequently until well
browned. Leave to cool and rub off the
skins before grinding.
• Many supermarkets and specialist food
stores sell flavoured coffees. Try using a
hazelnut-flavoured coffee for this dessert.

2 Put the ground coffee in a small bowl
and pour the water over. Leave to infuse
for 4 minutes, then strain through a fine
sieve. Place the hazelnuts in a coffee
grinder and grind until fine.

3 Peel, halve and core the pears. Thinly
slice across the pear halves part of the
way through, then brush them all over
with the orange juice.

4 Beat the butter and the larger quantity
of caster sugar together in a bowl until
very light and fluffy. Gradually beat in
the eggs. Sift the flour, then fold into the
mixture in the bowl. Add the hazelnuts
and coffee. Spoon the mixture into the
tin or soufflé dish, and level the surface.

5 Pat the pears dry on kitchen paper
and arrange in a circle in the sponge
mixture, flat side down. Brush them with
some of the maple syrup, then sprinkle
with the 15ml/1 tbsp caster sugar.

6 Cover the top of the tin or soufflé
dish with kitchen foil and place in the
ceramic cooking pot. Pour enough
boiling water around the tin or dish to
come slightly more than halfway up the
sides. Cover with a lid and cook for
3–3½ hours, until firm and well risen.

7 Meanwhile, make the orange cream.
Whip the cream, icing sugar and orange
rind until soft peaks form. Spoon into
a serving dish and chill until needed.

8 Leave the sponge to cool in the tin
for about 10 minutes, then turn over
on to a serving plate. Lightly brush
with the remaining maple syrup, then
decorate with orange rind and serve
with the orange cream.

Nutritional information per portion: Energy 852Kcal/3571kJ; Protein 12.5g; Carbohydrate 107g, of which sugars 45g; Fat 44.5g, of which saturates 23.8g; Cholesterol 169mg; Calcium 362mg; Fibre 5.3g; Sodium 493mg.

FRESH FRUIT BREAD and BUTTER PUDDING

Fresh currants add a tart touch to this scrumptious hot pudding. For the best results, use a wide, shallow dish rather than a narrow, deep one, but make sure it fits comfortably in the slow cooker. Serve drenched with a generous splash of fresh cream.

SERVES 4

40g/1½oz/3 tbsp butter, softened,
    plus extra for greasing
6 medium-thick slices of day-old bread,
    crusts removed
115g/4oz/1 cup prepared redcurrants
    and raspberries
3 eggs, beaten
50g/2oz/¼ cup golden caster
    (superfine) sugar
300ml/½ pint/1¼ cups creamy milk
5ml/1 tsp vanilla essence (extract)
freshly grated nutmeg
30ml/2 tbsp demerara sugar
single (light) cream, to serve

1 Generously butter a 1 litre/1¾ pints/ 4 cup round or oval baking dish – first checking that it fits in your slow cooker.

2 Pour about 2.5cm/1in of very hot water into the ceramic cooking pot. Place an upturned saucer or metal pastry ring in the base and switch the cooker to high.

3 Spread the slices of bread generously with the butter, then use a long serrated knife to cut them in half diagonally.

VARIATIONS
• Try using slices of Italian panettone in place of the white bread. It gives a particularly rich, indulgent result.
• Use fresh blueberries or blackcurrants in place of the fruit used here.
• When fresh berries and currants are unavailable, use chopped ready-to-eat dried apricots instead.

4 Arrange the buttered bread triangles in the dish in neat layers, overlapping the slices, with the buttered side facing up.

5 Scatter the fresh currants and berries over the bread and between the slices, ensuring that there is an even quantity of fruit throughout the pudding.

6 Place the eggs and caster sugar in a large mixing bowl and briefly beat together. Gradually whisk in the milk, vanilla essence and a large pinch of freshly grated nutmeg until well mixed.

COOK'S TIP
Always buy whole nutmegs. Once grated, the spice loses its flavour quickly.

7 Place the baking dish in the ceramic cooking pot, then slowly pour the egg and milk mixture over the bread, pushing the bread slices down to submerge them and making sure they are thoroughly soaked. Scatter the demerara sugar and a little nutmeg over the top, then cover the dish with foil.

8 Pour near-boiling water around the dish, so that the water level comes just over halfway up the sides of the dish. Cover with the lid and cook on high for 3–4 hours, or until a skewer inserted into the centre comes out clean.

9 Carefully remove the dish from the slow cooker and, if you like, briefly brown the top of the pudding under a hot grill (broiler). Cool slightly, then serve with the single cream.

Nutritional information per portion: Energy 405Kcal/1700kJ; Protein 12.6g; Carbohydrate 53.7g, of which sugars 30.7g; Fat 16.9g, of which saturates 8.6g; Cholesterol 202mg; Calcium 234mg; Fibre 2.1g; Sodium 405mg.

RICH CHOCOLATE CAKE

This rich, dense steamed chocolate cake filled with a decadently creamy buttercream makes a perfect teatime treat. Serve with a big cup of strong coffee.

SERVES 8

115g/4oz plain (semisweet) chocolate,
  chopped into small pieces
45ml/3 tbsp milk
150g/5oz/10 tbsp butter, at room
  temperature
200g/7oz/scant 1 cup soft light
  brown sugar
3 eggs, lightly beaten
200g/7oz/1¾ cups self-raising
  (self-rising) flour
15ml/1 tbsp (unsweetened) cocoa powder
icing (confectioners') sugar and
  (unsweetened) cocoa powder,
  for dusting

For the chocolate buttercream:
75g/3oz/6 tbsp butter, at room
  temperature
115g/4oz/1 cup icing (confectioners') sugar
15ml/1 tbsp (unsweetened) cocoa powder
2.5ml/½ tsp vanilla extract

1 Grease and line a deep 18cm/7in fixed-base cake tin (pan) or soufflé dish with baking parchment. Pour about 5cm/2in very hot water into the ceramic cooking pot, then turn the slow cooker to high.

2 Put the chocolate and milk into a heatproof bowl and place in the cooking pot. Leave for about 10 minutes, until the chocolate softens, then stir until smooth. Remove and leave to cool for a few minutes.

3 Meanwhile, place the butter and sugar in a mixing bowl and beat together until light and fluffy. Beat in the eggs, a little at a time, then stir in the chocolate mixture until well mixed.

4 Sift the flour and cocoa over the chocolate mixture and fold in until evenly mixed. Spoon into the prepared tin or dish and cover the top with a piece of foil. Put a saucer in the bottom of the ceramic cooking pot, then rest the tin on top. If necessary, pour in more boiling water to come just over halfway up the sides of the tin.

5 Cover the slow cooker with the lid and cook for 3–3½ hours, or until firm to the touch and a fine skewer inserted into the middle comes out clean. Carefully lift the tin out of the cooking pot and leave to stand on a wire rack for 10 minutes. Turn out and leave to cool. Remove the lining paper.

6 To make the buttercream, put the butter in a large bowl and beat until very soft. Sift over the icing sugar and cocoa powder, then stir together. Add the vanilla extract and beat until the buttercream is light and fluffy.

7 Very carefully, cut the cake in half horizontally and spread a thick, even layer of the buttercream on one of the cut halves. Sandwich the cakes back together, then dust with a mixture of icing sugar and cocoa and serve.

Nutritional information per portion: Energy 564Kcal/2363kJ; Protein 6.6g; Carbohydrate 70g, of which sugars 51g; Fat 30.5g, of which saturates 18.2g; Cholesterol 146mg; Calcium 129mg; Fibre 1.5g; Sodium 321mg.

CHOCOLATE CHIP WALNUT CAKE

The tangy flavour of orange works well in this chocolate and nut loaf. It can be finished simply with a generous dusting of icing sugar, or as here with a zesty orange topping.

SERVES 8

115g/4oz/1 cup plain (all-purpose) flour
25g/1oz/¼ cup cornflour (cornstarch)
5ml/1 tsp baking powder
115g/4oz/½ cup butter, at room temperature
115g/4oz/½ cup golden caster (superfine) sugar
2 eggs, lightly beaten
75g/3oz/½ cup plain (semisweet), milk or white chocolate chips
50g/2oz/½ cup chopped walnuts
finely grated rind of ½ orange

For the topping
115g/4oz/1 cup icing (confectioners') sugar, sifted, plus 5ml/1 tsp for dusting
20–30ml/4 tsp–2 tbsp freshly squeezed orange juice
walnut halves, to decorate

1 Grease and line a 450g/1lb loaf tin (pan), with a capacity of 900ml/1½ pints/ 3¾ cups, with baking parchment. Place a metal pastry ring or upturned saucer in the base of the ceramic cooking pot and pour in about 2.5cm/1in very hot water. Switch the slow cooker to high.

2 Sift the flour, cornflour and baking powder together twice, so that the dry ingredients are well mixed and aerated, then set aside.

3 Place the butter in a large mixing bowl and beat until creamy. Add the golden caster sugar and continue beating until light and fluffy. Add the eggs a little at a time, beating well after each addition.

4 Gently fold about half of the sifted flour mixture into the creamed butter and sugar mixture, then add the rest with the chocolate chips, walnuts and orange rind. Fold in until just blended, taking care not to overmix.

5 Spoon the mixture into the prepared loaf tin and loosely cover with a piece of foil, allowing some space at the top for the cake to rise as it cooks.

6 Put the loaf tin on the pastry ring or saucer inside the ceramic cooking pot. Pour enough boiling water around the loaf tin to come two-thirds of the way up the sides.

7 Cover the slow cooker with a lid and cook for 2½–3 hours, or until a fine skewer pushed into the centre of the cake comes out clean. Carefully remove the cake from the slow cooker and stand it on a wire rack for 10 minutes, then turn out and leave to cool on the rack.

8 To decorate the cake, place the 115g/4oz/1 cup icing sugar in a mixing bowl. Stir in 20ml/4 tsp of the orange juice, adding a little more if needed to make the consistency of thick cream. Drizzle the mixture over the cake, then decorate with walnut halves dusted with the 5ml/1 tsp icing sugar. Leave the topping to set before serving.

Nutritional information per portion: Energy 395Kcal/1655kJ; Protein 4.7g; Carbohydrate 51g, of which sugars 36.9g; Fat 20.5g, of which saturates 9.9g; Cholesterol 87mg; Calcium 49mg; Fibre 0.9g; Sodium 171mg.

FROSTED CARROT and PARSNIP CAKE

A delicious twist on the classic plain carrot cake, this version is wonderfully light and crumbly. The grated vegetables help to keep it moist, and account for its excellent keeping qualities. Cooked meringue spread over the top makes a change from the usual cream cheese topping, and makes a stunning contrast to the wholesome, crumbly cake.

SERVES 8

oil, for greasing
1 orange or lemon
10ml/2 tsp caster (superfine) sugar
175g/6oz/¾ cup butter or margarine
175g/6oz/¾ cup soft light brown sugar
3 eggs, lightly beaten
175g/6oz carrots and parsnips, grated
50g/2oz/⅓ cup sultanas
    (golden raisins)
115g/4oz/1 cup self-raising
    (self-rising) flour
50g/2oz/½ cup self-raising (self-rising)
    wholemeal (whole-wheat) flour
5ml/1 tsp baking powder

For the topping
50g/2oz/¼ cup caster (superfine) sugar
1 egg white
pinch of salt

1 Put an upturned saucer or metal pastry cutter in the base of the ceramic cooking pot and pour in about 2.5cm/1in hot water. Turn the slow cooker to high. Lightly grease a deep 18cm/7in round fixed-based cake tin (pan) or soufflé dish with oil and line the base with baking parchment.

2 Finely grate the orange or lemon rind, taking care not to take off any of the white pith. Selecting the longest shreds, put about half the rind in a bowl and mix with the caster sugar. Arrange the sugar-coated rind on a sheet of greaseproof (waxed) paper and leave in a warm place to dry.

3 Put the butter or margarine and brown sugar in a large mixing bowl and beat together until pale and fluffy. Add the eggs a little at a time, beating well after each addition. Stir in the unsugared orange or lemon rind, grated carrots and parsnips and sultanas.

4 Sift the flours and baking powder together, adding any bran left in the sieve (strainer), then gradually fold into the carrot and parsnip mixture.

5 Transfer the mixture to the prepared tin and level the surface. Cover loosely with greased foil, then place in the ceramic cooking pot, on top of the saucer or pastry cutter. Pour sufficient boiling water around the tin to come just over halfway up the sides.

6 Cover the slow cooker with the lid and cook for 3–5 hours, or until a skewer inserted in the centre of the cake comes out clean. Carefully lift the tin out of the slow cooker and leave to stand for 5 minutes. Turn the cake out on to a wire rack and leave until cool.

7 To make the topping, place the caster sugar in a bowl over the near-simmering water in the slow cooker. Squeeze the juice from the orange or lemon and add 30ml/2 tbsp of the juice to the sugar. Stir over the heat until the sugar dissolves. Remove from the heat, add the egg white and salt, and whisk for 1 minute with an electric beater.

8 Return the bowl to the heat and whisk for about 6 minutes until the mixture becomes stiff and glossy, holding a good shape. Remove from the heat and allow to cool for about 5 minutes, whisking frequently.

9 Swirl the meringue topping over the cake and leave for 1 hour to firm up. To serve, sprinkle with the sugared orange or lemon rind.

VARIATION
If you do not like parsnips, you can make this cake with just carrots, or replace the parsnips with the same weight of grated courgettes (zucchini). Add a pinch of cinnamon and nutmeg to the mixture.

Nutritional information per portion: Energy 410Kcal/1718kJ; Protein 5.9g; Carbohydrate 53g, of which sugars 38.2g; Fat 20.8g, of which saturates 12.2g; Cholesterol 132mg; Calcium 98mg; Fibre 1.9g; Sodium 290mg.

MOIST GOLDEN GINGER CAKE

This is the ultimate ginger cake: instead of the traditional black treacle, a mixture of golden syrup and malt extract gives a really sticky, moist texture. Because of the long slow cooking, the cake matures sufficiently to eat straight away. However, the flavour improves and the texture becomes stickier if it is wrapped and kept for a day or two.

SERVES 10

175g/6oz/generous ¾ cup light muscovado (brown) sugar
115g/4oz/½ cup butter
150g/5oz/⅔ cup golden (light corn) syrup
25g/1oz malt extract
175g/6oz/1½ cups self-raising (self-rising) flour
50g/2oz/½ cup plain (all-purpose) flour
10ml/2 tsp ground ginger
pinch of salt
1 egg, lightly beaten
120ml/4fl oz/½ cup milk, at room temperature
2.5ml/½ tsp bicarbonate of soda (baking soda)

1 Line the base of a deep 18cm/7in round fixed-base cake tin (pan) or soufflé dish with baking parchment. Pour 5cm/2in of very hot water into the ceramic cooking pot. Switch to high.

2 Place the sugar, butter, golden syrup and malt extract in a heatproof bowl that will fit inside the slow cooker. Place in the ceramic cooking pot and leave for 15 minutes, or until melted.

3 Remove the bowl from the slow cooker and stir until smooth. Place an upturned saucer or metal pastry ring in the base of the ceramic cooking pot.

4 Sift the flours, ginger and salt into a separate mixing bowl. Pour the melted butter and sugar mixture into the flour and beat until smooth. Stir in the beaten egg until well mixed.

VARIATION

To turn this moist cake into a tempting treat for kids, try decorating it with plain lemon icing (frosting) and scattering with multi-coloured sugar sprinkles. To make the icing, put 75g/3oz/¾ cup icing sugar in a bowl and stir in just enough lemon juice to make a smooth icing with the consistency of single (light) cream. Drizzle over the cake and scatter with sprinkles.

5 Pour the milk in a jug (pitcher) and stir in the bicarbonate of soda. Pour the mixture into the ginger cake mixture and stir until combined.

6 Pour the cake mixture into the prepared cake tin or soufflé dish, cover with foil and place in the cooking pot.

7 Pour a little more boiling water around the tin or dish to come just over halfway up the sides. Cover with the lid and cook for 5–6 hours, or until firm and a fine skewer inserted into the middle of the cake comes out clean.

8 Remove the cake from the slow cooker and place the tin or dish on a wire cooling rack. Leave to cool for 15 minutes, then turn out and leave to cool completely before serving in slices.

COOK'S TIP

Because this cake improves with keeping, it is the perfect choice when you are expecting guests because you can make it several days in advance.

Nutritional information per portion: Energy 289Kcal/1216kJ; Protein 3.4g; Carbohydrate 48g, of which sugars 31.1g; Fat 10.6g, of which saturates 6.4g; Cholesterol 48mg; Calcium 98mg; Fibre 0.7g; Sodium 211mg.

PRESERVES AND DRINKS

Although the slow cooker isn't suitable for fast-boiling jams, jellies and marmalades to setting point, it is perfect for making rich chutneys and relishes. The long, slow cooking develops their flavour to such an extent that long-maturation is unnecessary, and many can be eaten immediately. It is particularly good for making textured preserves, such as sweet and hot dried-fruit chutney, because the fruit and vegetables retain their shape well. Fruit curds, such as the traditional fresh lemon curd, are easier than those made conventionally because there is no need for constant stirring. You can also impress your Christmas guests with a home-made Christmas mincemeat – perfect for all those pies.

CARROT and ALMOND RELISH

This Middle Eastern classic, usually made with long fine strands of carrot, is available from many supermarkets. This version, using coarsely grated carrots, is just as good.

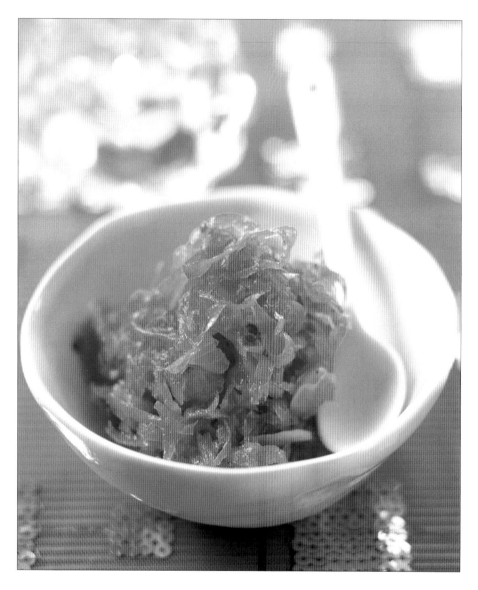

3 Switch the slow cooker to high and cook for about 2 hours, or until the carrots and ginger are almost tender, stirring only if the mixture looks dry around the edges.

4 Stir in the lemon rind and cook for a further 1 hour, until the mixture is thick. Stir once towards the end of the cooking time to prevent the mixture from sticking to the base of the pot.

5 Put the almonds in a frying pan and toast over a low heat until just beginning to colour. Gently stir into the relish, taking care not to break the almonds.

6 Spoon the relish into warmed sterilized jars, cover and seal. Store in a cool, dark place and leave to mature for 1 week. The relish will keep unopened for up to 1 year. However, once the jars have been opened, store them in the refrigerator and use within 2 weeks.

MAKES ABOUT 675g/1½lb

15ml/1 tbsp coriander seeds
500g/1¼lb carrots, grated
50g/2oz fresh root ginger, finely shredded
200g/7oz/1 cup caster (superfine) sugar
120ml/4fl oz/½ cup white wine vinegar
30ml/2 tbsp clear honey
7.5ml/1½ tsp salt
finely grated rind of 1 lemon
50g/2oz/½ cup flaked (sliced) almonds

1 Crush the coriander seeds using a mortar and pestle. Put them in the ceramic cooking pot with the carrots, ginger and sugar, and mix well.

2 Put the vinegar, honey and salt in a jug (pitcher) and stir until the salt has dissolved completely. Pour the mixture over the carrots. Mix well, cover and leave for 1 hour.

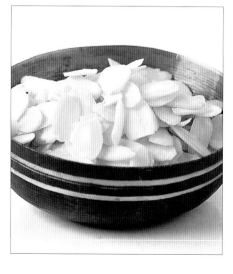

Nutritional information (total): Energy 1407Kcal/5947kJ; Protein 13.7g; Carbohydrate 289.6g, of which sugars 285.8g; Fat 29.4g, of which saturates 2.7g; Cholesterol 0mg; Calcium 268mg; Fibre 15.7g; Sodium 2898mg.

CONFIT of SLOW-COOKED ONIONS

This jam of slow-cooked, caramelized onions in sweet-sour balsamic vinegar will keep for several days in a sealed jar in the refrigerator. You can use red, white or yellow onions, but yellow onions will give the sweetest result. Shallots will also make an excellent confit.

2 Cover the pot with the lid, then place a folded dishtowel on top. Cook the onions for 5 hours, stirring the mixture several times during the cooking time to ensure the onions soften evenly.

3 Season well with salt and ground black pepper, then add the thyme, bay leaf, sugar, balsamic vinegar and red wine. Gently stir with a wooden spoon until the sugar has completely dissolved, then stir in the prunes.

4 Re-cover and cook for 1½–2 hours, or until the mixture is thick and sticky. Adjust the seasoning, adding more sugar and/or vinegar to taste. When cool, store the confit in the refrigerator. Serve either cold or warm.

SERVES 6

30ml/2 tbsp extra virgin olive oil
15g/½oz/1 tbsp butter
500g/1¼lb onions, thinly sliced
3–5 fresh thyme sprigs
1 bay leaf
30ml/2 tbsp light muscovado (brown)
    sugar, plus a little extra
30ml/2 tbsp balsamic vinegar,
    plus a little extra
120ml/4fl oz/½ cup red wine
50g/2oz/¼ cup ready-to-eat prunes,
    chopped
salt and ground black pepper

1 Put the oil and butter in the ceramic cooking pot and heat on high for about 15 minutes, until the butter has melted. Add the onions and stir to coat.

Nutritional information per portion: Energy 133Kcal/556kJ; Protein 1.2g; Carbohydrate 16.5g, of which sugars 14.6g; Fat 5.9g, of which saturates 1.8g; Cholesterol 5mg; Calcium 26mg; Fibre 1.6g; Sodium 20mg.

SWEET and HOT DRIED-FRUIT CHUTNEY

This rich, thick and slightly sticky preserve of spiced dried fruit is a wonderful way to enliven cold roast turkey left over from Christmas or Thanksgiving dinner.

MAKES ABOUT 1.5kg/3lb 6oz

350g/12oz/1½ cups ready-to-eat
   dried apricots
225g/8oz/1½ cups dried dates,
   stoned (pitted)
225g/8oz/1⅓ cups dried figs
50g/2oz/⅓ cup glacé (candied) citrus peel
150g/5oz/1 cup raisins
50g/2oz/½ cup dried cranberries
75ml/2½fl oz/⅓ cup cranberry juice
300ml/½ pint/1¼ cups cider vinegar
225g/8oz/1 cup caster (superfine) sugar
finely grated rind of 1 lemon
5ml/1 tsp mixed (apple pie) spice
5ml/1 tsp ground coriander
5ml/1 tsp cayenne pepper
5ml/1 tsp salt

1 Roughly chop the apricots, dates, figs and citrus peel, then put all the dried fruit in the ceramic cooking pot. Pour over the cranberry juice, stir, then cover with the lid and switch the slow cooker on to low. Cook for 1 hour, or until the fruit has absorbed most of the juice.

2 Add the cider vinegar and sugar to the fruit mixture. Turn the slow cooker up to the high setting and stir until the sugar has dissolved.

3 Re-cover and cook for 2 more hours, or until the fruit is very soft and the chutney fairly thick (it will thicken further as it cools). Stir in the lemon rind, mixed spice, coriander, cayenne pepper and salt. Cook uncovered for 30 minutes, until little excess liquid remains.

4 Spoon the chutney into warmed sterilized jars, cover and seal. Store in a cool, dark place. Open within 10 months of making. Once opened, store in the refrigerator and use within 2 months.

VARIATIONS
Pitted dried prunes can be substituted for the dates, and dried sour cherries for the dried cranberries. Apple juice can be used instead of the cranberry juice.

Nutritional information (total): Energy 2873Kcal/12248kJ; Protein 32g; Carbohydrate 714.3g, of which sugars 703.5g; Fat 6.8g, of which saturates 0.2g; Cholesterol 0mg; Calcium 1075mg; Fibre 52.1g; Sodium 2358mg.

BEETROOT, DATE and ORANGE PRESERVE

With its vibrant red colour and rich earthy flavour, this distinctive chutney is good with salads as well as full-flavoured cheeses such as mature Cheddar, Stilton or Gorgonzola.

MAKES ABOUT 1.4kg/3lb

300ml/½ pint/1¼ cups malt vinegar
200g/7oz/1 cup granulated sugar
350g/12oz raw beetroot (beets)
350g/12oz eating apples
225g/8oz red onions, very finely chopped
1 garlic clove, crushed
finely grated rind of 2 oranges
5ml/1 tsp ground allspice
5ml/1 tsp salt
175g/6oz/1 cup chopped dried dates

1 Put the vinegar and sugar in the ceramic cooking pot. Cover with the lid and switch the slow cooker to high. Leave until steaming hot.

2 Meanwhile, scrub or thinly peel the beetroot, then cut into 1cm/½in pieces. Peel, quarter and core the apples and cut into 1cm/½in pieces.

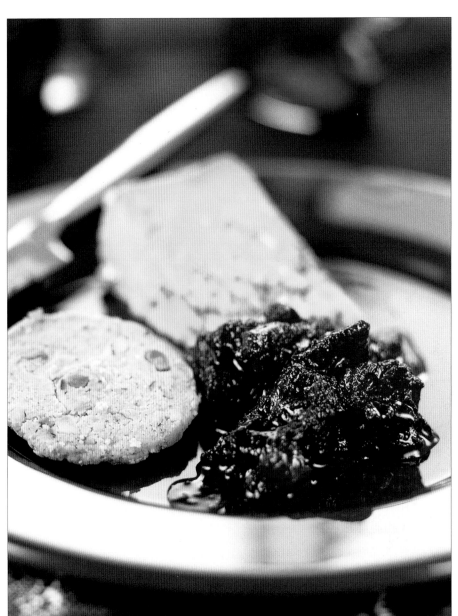

3 Stir the vinegar mixture with a wooden spoon until the sugar has dissolved. Add the beetroot, apples, onions, garlic, orange rind, ground allspice and salt. Stir everything together, then re-cover and cook for 4–5 hours, stirring occasionally until very tender.

4 Stir in the dates and cook for a further hour until the mixture is really thick. Stir once or twice during this time to prevent the chutney catching on the base of the ceramic cooking pot.

5 Spoon the chutney into warmed sterilized jars, cover and seal. Store in a cool, dark place and open within 5 months of making. Refrigerate after opening and use within 1 month.

COOK'S TIP
For really speedy preparation and a deliciously fine-textured chutney, put the peeled beetroot through the coarse grating blade of a food processor. Alternatively, you can simply grate the beetroot by hand.

Nutritional information (total): Energy 1632Kcal/6949kJ; Protein 16.8g; Carbohydrate 413.7g, of which sugars 406g; Fat 1.5g, of which saturates 0.2g; Cholesterol 0mg; Calcium 278mg; Fibre 23.1g; Sodium 2241mg.

FRESH LEMON CURD

This classic tangy, creamy curd is still one of the most popular of all the curds. Delicious spread thickly over freshly baked white bread or served with American-style pancakes, it also makes a wonderfully rich, zesty sauce spooned over fresh fruit tarts.

3 Put the eggs and yolks in a bowl and beat together with a fork. Strain the eggs into the lemon mixture, and whisk well until combined. Cover the bowl with foil, then return it to the slow cooker.

4 Cook the lemon curd on low for 1–2 hours, stirring every 15 minutes, until thick enough to lightly coat the back of a wooden spoon.

5 Pour the curd into small warmed sterilized jars. Cover and seal. Store in a cool, dark place, ideally in the refrigerator, and use within 3 months. Once opened, store in the refrigerator.

MAKES ABOUT 450g/1lb

finely grated rind and juice of 3 lemons
    (preferably unwaxed or organic)
200g/7oz/1 cup caster (superfine) sugar
115g/4oz/½ cup unsalted (sweet)
    butter, diced
2 large (US extra large) eggs
2 large (US extra large) egg yolks

COOK'S TIP
To make sharp, tangy lime curd, replace the lemons with the grated zest and juice of 4 large ripe, juicy limes. Lime curd has a lovely pale greenish hue.

1 Pour about 5cm/2in very hot water into the ceramic cooking pot. Switch the slow cooker to high. Put the lemon rind and juice, sugar and butter in the largest heatproof bowl that will fit inside the slow cooker.

2 Put the bowl into the slow cooker, then pour enough near-boiling water around it to come just over halfway up the sides. Leave for about 15 minutes, stirring occasionally, until the sugar has dissolved and the butter melted. Remove and allow to cool for a few minutes. Turn the slow cooker to low.

Nutritional information (total): Energy 1968Kcal/8224kJ; Protein 22.4g; Carbohydrate 215.3g, of which sugars 215.3g; Fat 118.9g, of which saturates 66.9g; Cholesterol 1102mg; Calcium 277mg; Fibre 0g; Sodium 895mg.

CHRISTMAS MINCEMEAT

In many mincemeat recipes, the raw ingredients are simply mixed together. Here, gentle cooking develops and intensifies the flavour, so that the mincemeat may be used straight away without being left to mature. At the same time, heating it to simmering point helps prevent fermentation, and this allows a much longer shelf-life.

MAKES ABOUT 1.75kg/4lb

450g/1lb cooking apples
115g/4oz/¾ cup glacé (candied) citrus peel
115g/4oz/½ cup glacé (candied) cherries
115g/4oz/½ cup ready-to-eat dried apricots
115g/4oz/1 cup blanched almonds
150ml/¼ pint/⅔ cup brandy
225g/8oz/1 cup currants
225g/8oz/1⅓ cups sultanas (golden raisins)
450g/1lb/3¼ cups seedless raisins
225g/8oz/1 cup soft dark brown sugar
225g/8oz/1⅔ cups suet (chilled, grated shortening) or vegetarian suet
10ml/2 tsp ground ginger
5ml/1 tsp ground allspice
5ml/1 tsp ground cinnamon
2.5ml/½ tsp grated nutmeg
grated rind and juice of 1 lemon
grated rind and juice of 1 orange

1 Peel, core and chop the cooking apples, then roughly chop the citrus peel, glacé cherries, apricots and blanched almonds.

2 Reserve half the brandy and put the rest into the ceramic cooking pot with all the other ingredients. Stir well until thoroughly mixed.

3 Cover the ceramic cooking pot with the lid and switch the slow cooker to high. Cook for 1 hour.

4 Stir the mixture well, then re-cover the pot and reduce the temperature to low. Cook for a further 2 hours, stirring halfway through cooking to prevent the mixture from overheating and sticking to the sides of the pot.

5 Remove the lid and leave the mixture to cool completely, stirring occasionally.

6 Stir the reserved brandy into the mincemeat and spoon the mixture into sterilized jars. Cover and store in a cool, dry place for up to six months. Once opened, store in the refrigerator and use within two weeks.

Nutritional information (total): Energy 7149Kcal/30087kJ; Protein 55.6g; Carbohydrate 1114g, of which sugars 1088.3g; Fat 267.7g, of which saturates 106.3g; Cholesterol 0mg; Calcium 1228mg; Fibre 47.3g; Sodium 774mg.

INDEX